AFTERBURN:

THE KC KOPASKA STORY

AFTERBURN:
THE KC KOPASKA STORY

A story of tragedy, redemption, and transformation.

Kc Kopaska

AND

Carole Liston

WestBow
PRESS
A DIVISION OF THOMAS NELSON

ISBN: 978-1-4497-1890-9 (sc)
ISBN: 978-1-4497-1891-6 (e)

Library of Congress Control Number: 2011931044

WestBow Press books may be ordered through booksellers or by contacting:

WestBow Press
A Division of Thomas Nelson
1663 Liberty Drive
Bloomington, IN 47403
www.westbowpress.com
1-(866) 928-1240

Printed in the United States of America

WestBow Press rev. date: 6/22/2011

NOTE TO READER:

This is a true story, based on true events.
It is a story of tragedy, redemption and transformation.
The extreme events described herein are at times painfully graphic, and the language is strong.

It is our purpose in sharing this story to inspire all who have endured life's traumas with a message of hope and the secrets to overcoming all the curve balls life can pitch your way.

We have endeavored to retain the story's authenticity without creating unnecessary offense. Every effort has been made to render Afterburn as a family-friendly book.

However, parents please be advised that some elements of this story may be unsuitable for young children. The story contains some strong language, graphic descriptions of physical trauma, and some graphic pictures.

Please use discretion in sharing this book with your children.

---Kc Kopaska and Carole Liston

WHAT OTHERS ARE SAYING....

"Kc's life is such a remarkable example of Christ's transforming power. I trust that this book will have a wide distribution and that those who read it will realize that Christ's transforming power is also available to them." ~ Dr. George Wood, General Superintendent, The General Council of the Assemblies of God

"This is a book that should be read by everyone. A well written testimony of God's Grace to one who has suffered more than many. KC Kopaska has surrendered to the will of God and lives it in his daily life. I am deeply move by his story. Extremely inspiring. He is a real Fire Chaplain." ~ Ed Stauffer, Director of the Federation of Fire Chaplains

"This kid doesn't stand a chance!" one Doctor said after observing this teenager burned over 60% of his body, But the painful path had a purpose and God used these black fibers within the tapestry of life to do a greater work. Horribly scarred on the outside, Kc ministers to those horribly scarred on the inside. Overcoming the grips of alcohol, drugs, depression, suicidal thoughts and loneliness, he is able to speak into the lives of the hurting and provide an everlasting hope. A must read! ~ Col (Ret) David G. Schall MD, MPH, FACS, FACPM

DEDICATION

It is the inner scars that cause the heart to cry. The outer ones are superficial in comparison. This book is dedicated to those that hold out the slimmest ray of hope that their crying hearts can once again sing songs of joy.

~ *Kc Kopaska*

TABLE OF CONTENTS

Chapter 1

UNTOUCHABLE

I was 17, blue eyed and rough cut; I thought I was ready for anything life could throw my way. During the school year, classes, wrestling, and bass guitar took up most of my time during the week. But on the weekends, it was time to party. I managed to mix a fair amount of the drugs and booze into the week, too. In spite of my zealousness for getting blasted out of my mind whenever possible, I remained physically strong for someone my size, in excellent physical condition, and felt untouchable. Life seemed like one big challenge just waiting to happen. Every day was an adventure, a new experience; the world was a big place and I wanted to see it all. I felt immune to accidents, serious injuries, or suffering. I was full of dreams and void of reality, unconcerned for consequences. As far as my eye could see, there was nothing ahead but a bright horizon, and my life was rising, like the morning sun. And now, shining on that bright horizon was the prospect of an entire summer in Colorado.

Chapter 2

SPLIT SECOND TO DESTINY

Virgil was a cowboy, a Colorado cowboy, body and soul hewn out of the majestic terrain of the Rocky Mountains and the demanding life of a high range rancher. Muscular and ruddy, he was the kind of a man who could toss a bale of hay like it was a loaf of bread. "A man can learn more by listening than talking," he once said, and he lived by that creed. He never trusted anyone who talked very much. Virgil had a good heart though, a genuine cowboy heart; he always offered a hand to help out a neighbor. I suppose that's why he befriended my aunt and uncle, Ann and Walt, when they moved from California to a nearby ranch, while others refused to help. And I suppose that's also why he agreed to give an Iowa kid like me a job as a ranch hand the summer I turned 17.

I first met Virgil when I had the good fortune to be invited to go on a hunting trip with my Dad and Walt in the fall of 1975. By this time, Walt and his wife had moved to Canon City, Colorado. Walt was married to my mom's Aunt Ann, both were in their mid-60s, still full of energy, still flavored with a strong twist of their ornery youth. Ann had been a fashion model when she was young and had a wicked temper; she either liked you or she didn't. Usually she didn't. Somehow I couldn't help but like her, though. Walt was a WW II vet with more tales of adventure than a Hollywood script. At seventeen he lied about his age to get into the Navy because his parents thought it was too dangerous to let him rodeo. He ended up having three ships sunk out from under him, including the Lexington. Ann didn't serve in WW II, but as ornery as she was, I always figured she probably started it.

When Walt invited my dad and me to go hunting in the Rockies, it was Virgil who opened up his land to us. He had a large tract of land and the idea was for us to hunt mule deer in the rugged scrub oak foothills just west of a little town called Wetmore, located about 35 miles southeast of Canon City. My little sister Carol came along for the ride. It was our first ever visit to the Rockies, quite a thrill for both of us, since the closest thing we had ever seen to a mountain was an Iowa haystack.

The first day of the hunt we met up with Virgil, who, despite his imposing appearance and quiet manners, went out of his way to accommodate our hunting expedition, guiding us to the best places to look for wild game on his land.

"I could sit up here forever," I thought to myself, perched atop the end of a long high ridge scouting for deer. The air was mountain fresh, little birds darted here and there, playing in the pines and scrub oak. We stalked game from morning to dusk from those high ridges. As twilight fell, I could see Wetmore nestled in among the hills, lights shimmering in the dusk. It sat tight against the foothills like a tiny gateway into the snow capped monoliths of the Sangre De Cristo mountains. I never did get a shot at a deer, but just sitting up there in those scrub oak and pine covered foothills, looking out over the great expanses to the south and the east while wild game passed by, was enough to lure me back. Little did I know as I gazed over this picturesque valley that my next trip to Wetmore would be a trip into a firestorm.

When the hunting expedition came to an end, we headed back to Iowa, but apparently Walt and Ann enjoyed our excitement and the exuberance of our youth. By Christmas, Carol and I had an invitation to come and spend the entire summer of 1976 with Walt and Ann. My parents said "yes." We were ecstatic.

The anticipation of spending the summer in the Colorado Rockies was just about more than I could bear. It was a dream come true for me – three months of adventure without parents screaming at me for every little thing I did, and every little thing I didn't do, either. My aunt and uncle were more open-minded than my parents, particularly about underage drinking, and that suited me just fine. It was exactly what I wanted, someone to loosen the reins and let me take the lead.

The first couple of weeks went well at Walt and Ann's, but I could not find enough to do around their place to keep me occupied and the La Damus' household was not about to let me freeload off of them. Besides, I needed to earn some spending money for the summer. Walt called Virgil to see if I could try out at his place as a ranch hand. The day before I was to start work, Walt took me out to his garage to look at a couple of pairs of his old chaps. Decked out in boots and a cowboy hat, Walt's chaps in hand, I headed out for work early, on the crisp, cool morning of June 14.

As I walked toward the door I looked back at Ann. She was sitting at the kitchen table sipping on her morning dose of milk and bourbon. I paused briefly, we swapped a few parting words, and then I left. The incident is hardly worth mentioning, except in hindsight. I recall this memory with an eerie sense of being in two places at once, not only walking out the door, but also sitting next to Ann at the table watching myself leave, 17-year-old "Kc Kopaska" as everyone knew him, myself included. The next time Kc walked back through that door he wouldn't be the same handsome young man he was when he left that day; in fact, he would never be the same again. Over the years, Ann often reminded me of that simple, everyday moment that became a turning point in all of our lives.

There was a cold, pine-scented wind blowing down out of the Rocky Mountain foothills that morning; it was invigorating as I headed for work, all decked out in leather chaps and a genuine cowboy hat. To the north, a snow capped Pike's Peak showed its golden colors in the post-dawn hours, while to the west the Sangre De Christos displayed their craggy peaks. Although the temperature had been in the 80s and 90s during the last two weeks, it was now closer to the mid-30s. I thought it was great weather for a first day on a hard-working ranch job, though.

Virgil met me when I pulled onto his Colorado ranch and we immediately headed out to a field in his truck, where my first assignment as summer ranch hand would be loading and unloading flatbed hay wagons. As to be expected, we didn't talk much on the way out to the field. This was cowboy territory, where entire rooms in houses are dedicated to trophies awarded with actions, not words – belt buckles, ribbons and prize saddles won in hard-fought rodeo competitions. It was all enough to keep my thoughts well occupied. There were tall boots to fill on this ranch and I was young, green, short, and straight from the cornfields of Iowa. When Virgil pulled his pickup truck through the fence gate and I came eyeball to eyeball with Frankie and Floyd, the two characters I would be working with for the day, I decided that keeping my mouth shut was definitely the best idea.

Frankie was taller and heftier than Floyd and looked about as intelligent as the bale of hay he was standing near. Floyd was a scrawny kid, my age, who looked like he was just full of it. But they were experienced ranch hands, and they were friends. I was the new kid on the block. If anything was for certain, it was that they would test me, and it wasn't going to take long for it to begin.

After the three of us loaded the first wagon, we were hauled, along with it, to a pole barn that had no sides, but only a corrugated metal roof to keep the rain and winter snow off of the hay we were stacking inside. It was still morning and the idea was for the three of us to unload the wagon, go have lunch, and then head back out to the field. I didn't catch what was going on at first, but Frankie and Floyd were dragging their feet real slowly to get the hay off the wagon. Now one thing I knew a lot about was working hay. I had baled tons of it, summer after Iowa summer. But in Iowa, we worked a whole lot faster and harder than these two nuts, who were slower than cold molasses. Finally, Virgil was back in his work truck and pulled up closely to check on us.

"Hey, how come you guys don't have this wagon unloaded yet?" he yelled. Frankie immediately turned to him and responded, "Oh – it's Kc. He's not used to the hay dust. It's messin' with his eyes and we couldn't work too fast." I was dumbfounded by this total lie, but didn't know what to do about it. So I did the obvious – nothing. Looking back on it, I wish I would have gone ahead and hit Frankie right between the eyes and knocked the snot out of him. I was too naïve to realize they were trying to get me fired on the first day of the job.

By the time we had the hay neatly stowed away in the barn, it was time for noon break. Virgil asked me if I wanted to go to lunch with him. The logical thing to do would have been for me to say "yes" so that I could get to know my new boss a little better, and find out what effect Frankie's lame excuse for not getting the wagon unloaded had on his view of me. Instead, I made the dumbest decision of my life and turned him down so that I could have lunch with my newfound "friends."

Everything went surprisingly well. Even though they put the finger on me with their first little scheme, my keep-your-mouth-shut instincts paid off. We actually got along quite well at lunch. They were full of the pride and imagination of youth and so was I. There was still some sizing up to do, and bragging rights to establish. It all seemed well worth passing up a free lunch with Virgil.

The hay barn was across the street from the Wetmore Bar and Grill. We headed over there for lunch, but the kitchen was closed, so we settled for a couple of games of pool instead. I won. I wasn't better than them, just luckier...but they didn't need to know that. Not today.

Needing to eat, we moved to the grocery store and bought some nutritious and delicious bologna and bread for sandwiches, then made our way down the old highway heading north out of town to find a spot to pull over and eat. Frankie was driving a one-ton truck with a flatbed on the back and Floyd and I were in Virgil's Willys Jeep. We parked side by side in a drive facing an open field, across from a house where, according to Floyd, lived a beautiful young girl, just about our age.

Floyd and I climbed into the truck with Frankie and as we sat there and chewed on our sandwiches we talked the talk of teenage boys obsessed with a powerful urge to breed with anything resembling the other gender. Though nothing was out of the ordinary, I had a strange sense about that moment, a part of me just wanted to hold onto it a little longer. Believe me, it wasn't because of the cowboys. Even though we needed to get back to work, I just did not want to hurry away from this place. There was nothing special about it at all. It was just a field, an old truck, and three idiots who knew nothing about girls, telling each other everything they knew about nothing. Finally, we were done eating, I brushed this odd feeling aside, and we headed back to the field. Frankie took off ahead of Floyd and me in the truck, while we followed in the Jeep. Floyd, of course, was driving.

The doors had been taken off of the Jeep and as we traveled down the old road, Frankie already out of sight, the fresh mountain air was blowing in through the Jeep. It felt good as we meandered along. Floyd asked me if I chewed and pulled a bag of Red Man chewing tobacco out of his shirt pocket. No way was I going to say "no," so I took a pinch and stuck it in between my cheek and gums.

"Aw, come on, is that all you're gonna take?" he half questioned, half challenged.

"Give me some more of that!" I shot back. This time I shoved a great big wad in my mouth and began a slow deliberate chew on it. Very slow. I wasn't new to chewing tobacco, but I just wasn't very good at it, especially the most important part of it: spitting.

As Floyd and I traveled along, I glanced down at the new pair of leather gloves in my lap and felt a strong urge to go ahead and put them on. "Why put those gloves on yet?" I asked myself. "They're bulky and stiff. We're not even out to the field yet." I resisted the urge and left the gloves sitting where they were. I was just about to unload a hefty volley of saliva and tobacco juice when Floyd's cowboy hat flew off his head and landed in the Jeep directly behind him. Instinctively, he reached back to grab it. As he twisted his body, he unwittingly pulled the steering wheel hard to the left. The Jeep headed for the ditch.

"Hey! You're going for the ditch!" I yelled as the Jeep veered off the road on the wrong side of the highway. In a flash, things went from bad to worse. The Jeep, without slowing, took dead aim on a telephone pole. "Telephone pole!" I screamed.

Floyd panicked. He meant to mash the brake but he missed and hit the accelerator instead. The Jeep swerved to the right as he jerked the steering wheel and skyrocketed out of the ditch, landing hard on the pavement. Unbeknownst to either of us, someone had placed a Jerry can full of gasoline inside of the Jeep and neglected to tie it down. All of the jarring knocked it open as it bounced around inside of the tiny vehicle. As we careened from ditch to ditch, the gasoline had been splashing, soaking into my clothes, running down my right side, my back, and the back of my jeans. I was a torch waiting to be lit.

Floyd was fighting hard to regain control of the Jeep, but the bucking vehicle would not be tamed. It took its own diagonal course across the highway toward the ditch on the right hand side of the road. Suddenly, I smelled gasoline.

Out of fear of an explosion, I grabbed the handle on the dashboard with my left hand and the back of the seat with my right, and prepared to bail out. Just as I was going to leap, the Jeep hit the ditch, and time suspended. Somehow, the combined forces of impact vaulted the Jeep into the air, sailing over the barbed wire fence that paralleled the road. I was looking down out of the Jeep, still wanting to jump, but as we cleared the top strand of the fence I thought to myself, "If I jump now I'll get my throat cut." For a split second, I hesitated. Precisely then, somewhere in mid-air, the gasoline found its way to a spark.

The Jeep exploded.

Chapter 3

DEFINED BY FIRE

Whoosh! The massive explosion of energy ignited with a thunderclap of sound and flame. The sound of flammable liquids igniting was familiar to me, but always before it had been a noise that came from a direction away from me, usually because I did something risky, like squirt lighter fluid or gasoline on hot coals before tossing a match into the vapor it created. The sound was always one-dimensional. It came from a single direction.

This time it was different.

Now, it was "surround-sound" and I was consumed by it. It came from every direction. The gasoline and its vapors excited the flames. I was immersed in a hellish, catastrophic eruption, as fierce as vengeance. For a moment my entire world was defined by fire, bright orange flames engulfed the inside of the Jeep. Out of instinct I yelled, "JUMP!" and hurled myself out of the inferno as the Jeep hit the ground on the other side of the fence.

It was too late.

My gasoline-soaked clothing took over where the Jeep explosion left off. Though I hit the ground rolling, hoping to extinguish the flames, the fire just kept roaring. I didn't realize it at the time, but I was rolling in a dry, grassy pasture. With every roll, my flaming body was setting the field on fire, adding to the searing heat. Nature dealt her own cruel blow by mercilessly fanning the flames with that cold morning wind, which moments before had seemed to be my best friend. Now that same mountain wind became my worst enemy, charging down out of the mountains and onto the neighboring plains, fanning the incessant flames.

Still, I kept rolling. The fire would not give up its relentless assault on my dying flesh. I became angry. I suddenly had an awareness that it was eating my face away. My thoughts raced for a solution.

"Damn this fire! It's messing me up!" I rolled with both hands over my face in a vain attempt to protect my youthful good looks. It was of little use. Time himself seemed to slow down to watch the gruesome spectacle. Everything went into slow motion as I fought the fire. Roll. Whoosh! The gasoline soaked clothes on my backside would ignite as I rolled on my stomach. Roll. Whoosh! My front side re-ignited when I rolled on my back again. It was a mad cycle of torment and rapidly increasing hopelessness. Then I became furious. This had to stop. But how?

Suddenly, in a flash, I knew the answer. I could stop fighting and give my life to the fire. In a brief moment of clarity, my mind laid before me a choice. "I can inhale this fire, give myself up to it and die right now, or I can fight through this and live, but never be the same person again." I had no concept or concern about what might lie on the other side of death. As far as I knew, there would be no pain, no suffering, my life would just cease to be. If I took one breath of the flames, it would be all over. The same element that was mauling my skin with its fiery teeth would make quick work of my fragile lungs.

Time stopped altogether now, as if holding his breath – watching me, waiting to see what I would choose.

A thought came unbidden to my mind, as if Someone was giving me a choice. "So, you choose. Will it be life or will it be death?"

Death. In an instant, I knew.

I chose death.

I stood in the flames and exhaled all the air out of my lungs, prepared to breathe in the fire. Perched on the threshold of eternity, I was literally one breath away from stepping over. Then as I chose death, for reasons beyond my understanding, a remarkable thing happened. Life chose me. Darkness intervened.

With no sense of falling, I felt the ground rise up to meet me. A black quiet washed over me like a flood. I knew that I hit something, but there was no pain, in fact, there was no feeling of any kind, only the dark intruding world of the unconscious.

Unconsciousness was replaced by peace when I emerged from my involuntary slumber. It was a euphoric kind of peace that saturated my entire being. I did not feel the ground, even though I was lying on it. Neither did I feel any pain or any other sensation, for that matter. Fear was a thousand galaxies away harassing some other poor soul. All that I could feel physically, emotionally and mentally was pure, inexpressible peace. Lying there on the horizon between the black void of unconsciousness and the blinding light of reality, a Voice spoke to me. It was clear, it was inner, and it was Other.

"Everything is going to be alright."

My euphoric state shattered.

I awoke a different man. Whereas before I was ready to give up and die, suddenly I was fueled by an irresistible urge to fight and survive. I opened my eyes, stood up, and looked around. I was no longer on fire and the field had quit burning, but the Jeep was still a roaring ball of flames. Puzzled by a big chunk of substance stuck in my cheek I spit hard toward the ground. Out popped the wad of Redman tobacco I had crammed into my cheek just moments before the accident. I almost laughed.

"Where's Floyd?" I wondered and began desperately looking. Then I saw him. He was walking around from the other side of the Jeep with his arms held straight out in front of him like a zombie.

"What are we going to do? What are we going to do," he kept repeating, in a trancelike state. To this day I don't remember what his body looked like. I don't know why. I remember every other detail of the accident. Maybe it's a mercy that my mind won't let me recall this.

"Floyd, lie down. I'll get help," I said. Still no response.

"What are we going to do? What are we going to do," he repeated again, looking right through me. Floyd gave no trace of recognition, as if I wasn't there.

Instantly I understood that any help from Floyd was out of the picture. The only possibility of our survival would depend on me finding a way to get us to a hospital. Burned beyond recognition, I was an unlikely hero. But quickly scanning the countryside, I spotted a ranch house about a quarter of a mile away to the northeast of where I was standing. It was the nearest place I could see; in fact, it was the only place I could see. I was losing vision fast. I turned my back on Floyd and started walking.

As I made my way through the field, I made sure to keep my eyes on the ground so as not to trip over something and fall. The skin on my hands and fingers was hanging in yellowish shreds like the skin on a boiled chicken. I did not want to catch myself with my hands if I should stumble. Besides, my range of focus continued narrowing as tunnel vision from shock set in.

When I first started walking toward the house I was walking on charred grass, but I had only taken a few steps before I was walking on dry weeds again, uncharred. It puzzled me. The wind was at my back, which meant that the fire should have kept burning in the same direction I was walking. As strange as it seemed that a wind-driven fire would stop burning so abruptly, I gave it no further thought until much later. At the time, there was only one thing on my mind – get to the house, get help. Halfway across the field, it still seemed like a marathon to that destination of hope.

Through my blurry vision I could see the house approaching. I wasn't in much pain at this point, though my hands were beginning to hurt. A full thickness burn mercifully seals the nerve endings, so no pain registers for a while. I had no idea how extensive my burns were, but as bad as my hands looked, my body was far worse. I was a walking mass of third degree burns. Most of my clothes had been completely burned off except where the leather chaps and my boots had covered my legs and feet. My head, including my entire face, neck, torso, arms, hands, my buttocks and the back of my legs about halfway down to the knees had been thoroughly cooked. I was a walking pork chop, well done to a crackly crunch.

Finally, I approached a large steel gate just across the drive from the house which was, much to my relief, already open. As soon as I stepped through my heart nearly leapt to my throat in a wave of panic as I thought, "What if no one is home? What then? What will I do if no one is home?"

The short walk from the gate to the house seemed like miles instead of yards. The closer I got to the screen door that represented our only hope for survival, the harder my heart pounded in my chest. As I stepped up onto the concrete porch and began to bang on the door, panic gave way to unbending determination. I would get into that house even if I had to tear the whole thing down to the foundation.

Because of the shape my hands were in, I reared back and let a hard kick fly with one of my boots to the tin storm door. "OPEN UP!" I yelled. "There's been an accident!" No answer.

"Open the door! We need help!" I yelled again. In desperation, I began to kick the door in. Finally a very frightened little boy peered through the door and opened it. He and his brother were the only ones home. One was about eight, the other, 11 years old.

I have often wondered if they had observed the accident and watched in horror as Floyd and I flailed around in the field like two Hollywood stuntmen jumping out of a burning car for a cheering crowd. But we weren't stuntmen. There was no cheering crowd. And there was no one around with fire extinguishers to put us out. Our audience consisted of two little boys traumatized by a sight no person should have to see. Perhaps that is why it took them so long to open the door.

"We've been in an accident. Call an ambulance," I said. As soon as the words came out of my mouth, one of the boys picked up the phone and called the fire department. "No! Call an ambulance!" I repeated. It really didn't matter. After the boy made the phone call, I looked to the right into a mirror on an antique buffet and saw myself. I was smoldering.

"Can you put me out?" I asked. "I need a bathtub of water or a hose." The younger brother led me to a water hydrant outside, just off the porch, and turned it on for me. The cool water splashing against my smoldering flesh felt good. After a liberal dousing there wasn't much left to do but wait for help to arrive.

From the porch, I could see activity beginning around the scene of the accident. A couple of people had arrived but I couldn't recognize them. They were looking all around for something. I finally figured out that they were probably looking for me and sent one of the boys over to get them. As soon as he got their attention, they came running across the field. It was Virgil and Frankie. Frankie had seen the smoke in his rearview mirror and had turned around to see what it was all about. How Virgil knew, I have no idea, but I wasn't surprised. Virgil was a true cowboy, and had a sense about his land; he could smell trouble. I was still sitting on the porch when they dashed through the gate. Judging by the looks on their faces, they didn't seem to be too happy about the condition I was in. Their expressions were a mixture of fear and astonishment.

The rescue squad from Florence was speeding to the scene by this time, and I asked Frankie to cut my chaps off, which he did by slicing through the belt with his pocket knife. He and Virgil didn't know what to do for me, so I told them to go get a sheet wet and hold it over me to keep the sun off of my burned skin. I highly doubt the sheet did me any good physically, but it made me feel good to think I was in charge and giving orders in the situation. When the paramedics arrived and began prepping me for transport, I looked up to what seemed a very tall highway patrol officer standing over me jotting notes on some sort of writing pad. The whole time he was writing he kept shaking his head back and forth as if to say, "This kid doesn't have a chance."

I ignored him. Now that I had begun to fight, there was a powerful lot of fight packed into this little dog.

Virgil tried to help lift me onto the gurney and get me into the ambulance by placing his hands under my shoulders. As he did, a large chunk of skin from my left shoulder sloughed off into his hand.

"Damn it, Virgil! Don't you know you're not supposed to grab me that way?!" I yelled.

To be honest, it didn't hurt, and my anger wasn't personal. I knew Virgil was only trying to help. I just felt like cussing at the moment. So I did. A lot.

In the ambulance on the way to the hospital, I just wanted to lie quietly, undisturbed. I did not want to talk. I did not want to tell the paramedics what day it was, or where I was. I just wanted to rest. Suddenly, I was tired. Then they started in on me. The two medics in the back of the ambulance began pestering me with questions and would not let up.

"What day is it?" One of them asked.

"Who cares, leave me alone," I answered.

"Where are you?" The other one asked.

"Kiss my ass," I said.

Then another question, and another. They would not stop. They were trained not to let me slip into the sleep of shock, so the questions kept rolling. Finally, I lit up with a fury that made the burning Jeep pale in comparison.

Straining against the gurney straps with every ounce of energy I had left, I began yelling at the top of my lungs. "Idiots! Shut up or I'll kill you both!" I screamed. "If I get out of these straps, you'd be better off dead!!!!" I then let off the finest, longest blue streak of cuss words in the English language, threatening them with so much vigor that they literally backed up to the far corner of the ambulance, a look of complete astonishment pasted on both of their faces.

They looked afraid that I might actually break the straps loose! Thank God I didn't. I still had my boots on and I was mad enough that I would have kicked the stuffing out of both those guys in a heartbeat. Now it was my turn not to let up. They heard it all the way to the hospital. Before the ride was over, the paramedics were the ones in shock, I can guarantee it.

Finally, we arrived at the hospital in Florence, where an unknown doctor practicing in a tiny community hospital met that "Great Challenge" which professors of medical students promise will someday come to each of them, just when they least expect it and often when they feel least prepared to handle it. The "Great Challenge" is a medical emergency of extraordinary proportion that falls into their lap, unannounced, when there is no one else to take charge. On that day, they will have no choice but to be the point man or woman in the situation; on that day they will be fully tested as a physician; and on that day the quality of their practice of medicine will make a life-and-death difference for some poor soul caught up in the battle to survive.

Today was that day for Dr. Berge. It was his moment; and he stepped into it. He grabbed what little was available to him and set to work to save our lives.

Chapter 4

PROGNOSIS: GRAVE

(Florence Hospital)

"The patient arrived at the emergency room at approximately 4:55 p.m. with second and third degree burns involving 70-80% of his body. Vital signs were not able to be obtained because of the severity of the burns on his arms. The patient's appendages about the head, including the ears, nose, eyelashes, eyebrows and lips were markedly burned, swollen, and peeling. The patient's extremities were already beginning to swell markedly; there were extensive burns to the trunk as well. IVs were started on the patient, a nasogastric tube was inserted, a Foley catheter was inserted and burned areas were covered with large amounts of Silvadine cream. A subclavian catheter was used for fluid therapy; Demurral morphine.

"Within an hour, because of marked swelling involving both arms in which skin became parchment-like, a fasciotomy incision of both arms was done at about 6:20 p.m. Initial attempts to transfer the patient to Denver proved futile, since there was no bed available at the burn unit in Denver. Contacts were then made with Brooke Army Hospital in San

Antonio, Texas, and with the Air Force transportation unit located in Illinois. Arrangements were finally made for the patient to be transferred to San Antonio, Texas, and to be taken to Pueblo Airport where he was to be picked up by an Army Medical Transport jet at 11:30 p.m. The patient therefore was prepared and transferred by Andrews Ambulance at approximately 10 p.m. Almost the patient's entire body was covered by Silvadine, kerlix, and sterile sheets.

"By the time of his transfer, he was resting fairly quietly, but with prognosis of his survival grave." (Dr. Berge, hospital notes, the Florence Hospital medical records)

I continued cussing steadily into the emergency room, only now I was cussing the increasing pain that was beginning to wrack every inch of my body. Floyd was lying on the table next to me, but he wasn't making a sound. I wondered if my Uncle Walt was at the hospital yet, and asked if he could come in and see me. He was brought to the ER. As he bent down over me, I could only see his face dimly, but it gave me a great sense of comfort. With a weak voice I said, "Well, Walt, I guess I got myself into a real mess this time."

"You sure did, Kc," Walt answered. I don't recall anything else being said between us. The morphine was beginning to take hold. I felt like going to sleep.

Things were not looking good, and not everything at the hospital went smoothly. Medical personnel and first responders are often themselves severely stressed by critical incidents, and sometimes say things that they may later regret. The Florence Hospital, designed for routine care in a small community of less than 3,000, rarely dealt with such unfathomable injuries as ours. An attending nurse blurted out to my aunt and sister, "I wouldn't give you a plug nickel for those boys' lives." They were devastated. According to his medical notes, Dr. Berge must have felt the same way, but to his credit he kept this opinion to himself. Instead, he fought for our lives as if we had every chance of survival. Regardless of the prognosis, Dr. Berge practiced "possibility" medicine – he determined to give us every possibility of living. The odds of survival were simply not in my favor except for the fact that it was God who had the last say in the matter. He had given me a promise in that field that everything would be alright. He keeps his promises.

When Dr. Berge had done all he could do to stabilize us, he called the burn unit in Denver, but he was a little too late. The two beds they had available earlier in the day were now filled. That's when he decided to try Brooke Medical Burn Unit at Fort Sam Houston in San Antonio, Texas. An army hospital, it was considered the best burn unit in the world at the time. Incredibly, two beds had become available in their intensive care just that day. One can only wonder what would have become of Floyd and me if we had been sent to Denver. It didn't matter for Floyd, anyway. He didn't make it out of Brooke alive.

Chapter 5

GROWING UP FREE

Lush green cornfields, along with the remnants of the last virgin prairie of Central Iowa, a few old houses and some broken down buildings were what was left of a town called Crocker – the place I called "home." At one time, like many small farm communities in America, Crocker had been a thriving center of commerce. By the time we moved there in 1964, however, this little dot on the Iowa prairie consisted of only eight houses, one of them abandoned and rumored to be haunted, an old, defunct church, and the shell of a grocery store, now just an extra building attached to the Voshells' place.

But for the 26 kids that lived in Crocker, summers seemed to have been "made in heaven." Hot steamy days were swallowed up by the play we created through the use of our active, unspoiled imaginations, while dancing sun rays bleached our hair and baked our skin into an envious tan. Life was never, ever lonely. Every day my brothers and sisters and I ran with the pack of "... all those damned neighbor kids in Crocker," as my dad called them. In fact, kids hung together so well, that it seemed like most of the kids in Crocker lived together from house to house, pretty much all summer long. The parents probably would have preferred other arrangements, since this meant having all 26 kids at your house at one time, none of them well behaved. But that's how we lived.

To be straight up honest, Crocker was a classic case study in family and social dysfunction. It was dysfunctional, yes, but at the same time it was what a lot of people consider "normal" in small-town, rural America. Dysfunctional or not, no place beat Crocker for summertime fun. Crocker was a gritty place, where kids made their own fun, and a lot of it was trouble. If we weren't inside the houses driving someone's parents crazy, you could bet we were outside, creating havoc, and having a great time doing it.

There were always plenty of "community activities" to keep us occupied in Crocker. Throwing rocks and eggs at the cars zooming by on the highway was one. Another was shooting out the windows of the new cars riding piggy back on the rail cars that rumbled past our little community. We even had a tourist attraction in our little town: Crocker's very own "haunted" house.

For starters, the abandoned house was deemed "haunted" by unanimous agreement of all 26 kids. All abandoned houses in small isolated communities are haunted, of course, a scientific fact that nearly all kids understand on a very gut level. Somebody once rented that old house and charged people money to walk through one Halloween, deep in the October dark. We local kids didn't go in, though. We knew what evil lurked in the dark corners of that devil's lair. There were stairs that were creaky and old and rusty hinges that screamed in the night. But the real horror of the abandoned house was found in the piles of raccoon poop strewn several inches deep from wall to wall. A kid could get used to the creaks of the stairs and the screams of the hinges, but raccoon poop squishing between your toes? Even the thought made us shudder. That was enough to quiver the liver of the bravest of kids.

We may have been creative, but we were sorely lacking in "character training." In fact, the only "character training" we received was imitating some of the adult "characters" that lived in Crocker. There was no YMCA or Boys and Girls Club, or anything remotely like them. Left to ourselves and our adult role models, we fought, drank, smoked and got high, and that was just in our prepubescent years. When we ran out of trouble we could get into in Crocker, then we headed to the next larger town, Polk City, to terrorize whomever and whatever was unfortunate enough to cross our path. Out of all 26 kids, well over half grew up to be serious substance abusers. A very significant number also became alcoholics. I was 12 years old when I started down that road myself.

There were some interesting adult role models living in Crocker, though, and I am sure that all of them, in one way or another, helped to warp our little lives. First, there was "Bun" Beason, chosen to be the unofficial Mayor of Crocker. His house was surrounded by three abundantly producing apple trees, whose fruit he mostly used to make wine. I harvested his apples, too, for my own uses – to throw at cats, dogs, and other neighbor kids. He was as ugly as a mud fence, but with a name like "Bun" I figured there was an easy explanation; he looked like he must have fought a whole lot growing up. What kind of a twisted parent names his kid "Bun," anyway?

Then there was Louise Argetsinger who lived next door to Bun with her four boys, one daughter, and a husband named Homer. Louise both loved and hated the Kopaska kids. Well, actually, she just loved to hate us. She loved us when we left town and hated us when we came back. I didn't always like her much, either. She got my hide severely tanned one day by squealing on us for burying the Danielsons' cats. They lived next door to Louis. Evidently, she did not see the humor in burying cats while they were still breathing. Judging by the cats' reaction, they didn't see much humor in it, either.

Larry Danielson's property bordered Louis'. Larry was the village idiot. We didn't care what he thought of us, though I am sure he thought of us quite often. He thought of us kids in his nightmares, he thought of us when he was slogging down a fifth of vodka, and I'm sure, quite often, he thought of us when he was cleaning his gun.

One day Larry got the bright idea of adding to his personal torment (and ours) by becoming the school bus driver for the kids from Crocker! Who would want that job? The devil himself wouldn't have wanted to drive the Crocker kids' school bus. Larry didn't seem to be quite as smart as the devil, though. So we drove him crazy on that bus. On one occasion he got so perturbed at us that he brought the bus to a screeching halt right on the highway and ordered every one of us to get off, including his own two daughters.

"Just get OFF this bus, damn it!! Stupid, smart-mouth kids!" he ordered. "Find your OWN way home, each and every one of you!" And he seriously meant it. He dropped us off by the road back to Crocker and drove off. We had to find our own way home.

After a moment of complete shock, we began to whoop and holler.

It was our crowning achievement, our greatest legacy. Never before in the history of the Ankeny school system had so many kids been kicked off of a single bus, all at the same time. Larry nearly lost his job over that ordeal.

He was already in the process of losing his mind. He shot his wife straight through the foot with a handgun one night. Honest. We always thought he must have had his gun too close by his bed when he woke up from a bus driving nightmare and mistook her for one of us!

I could go on and talk about Calvin Voshell who, with clenched teeth, swore he would never again "...grow another damn watermelon for those damn kids to haul out of his damn garden, damn it!" People cussed a lot in Crocker.

Then there was also "Old Lady Benson" who lived by the highway with her two pretty daughters and a double barrel shotgun that she kept right by the door, for reasons obvious to her and all the boys in Crocker, too. But enough reminiscing about the town's colorful cast of characters. What was best about Crocker could be summed up in one phrase: the "Great Outdoors," and the freedom to explore it.

The Great Outdoors was definitely what I liked most about growing up in Crocker. Besides my brothers, Craig Argetsinger was one of the people I shared it with the most, which might be one of the reasons his mom Louise was not so very fond of me. As far back as I can remember, I liked being outside so much that on hot summer nights after the lights were all out and no one was stirring, I would sneak out of bed, put on my clothes, and head outside to play. Usually, I would throw rocks at Craig's window until he got up and came out to play with me. On many of those nights, he would already be outside, camping in his backyard pup tent. Sometimes, in the pale light of a full moon, we would walk the old railroad tracks that ran by our place and just talk.

The nature of our discussions was as limitless as the starry sky. These talks were rare moments that allowed the naïve minds of two young boys to explore the meaning of life, unencumbered by politics, religion, or economics; to develop a simple philosophy of life that was untainted by the complexities of the adult world. If Craig had his tent up, we would lay on our backs, top half of our bodies outside the tent, hands clasped together behind our heads, gazing at the stars for hours. We mused about anything, everything, and sometimes nothing at all; nothing except silver dots of light, shooting stars, and imaginary civilizations so very far away yet so very real in our minds.

I liked Craig a lot. He was a once-in-a-lifetime friend, and I always left our times together feeling good about him. That is, all except for the time he tried to kill me.

It was winter, the morning after a snowstorm, and the sharp cold air and azure blue sky felt clean and inviting. The fresh white landscape glistened like jewels in a Saudi Arabian palace. The snow drifted high along the fence in our back yard and Craig and I were crawling around in some tunnels that a bunch of us kids had burrowed in our day's play. As it began to get later in the afternoon, Craig's dad Homer came outside and began calling for Craig to come home. Craig laughed at the thought that we could see his dad from inside one of our tunnels, but he could not see us.

"Craig! Craig! Come on home!" His father yelled. Instantly, it became a game to us, to see if he could find us. Instead of coming out, all we did was laugh. Craig's dad yelled louder, and we laughed louder.

Soon we fell flat on our backs. "Hoo-ha, Hoo hoo Ha," we gasped.

"Craig, Craig where are you?" his dad wailed. And as he did, our laughter grew into side splitters.

"Hoo-hoo-hoo-haah-haah-haah," we roared.

Then the game backfired on Craig. He laughed too hard. So hard, in fact, that his bladder gave way under the strain and he completely soaked his britches! In a flash, his laughter turned to humiliation and with no warning at all he kicked in the top of our tunnel to cover his mishap with snow. This may have been a perfect way for him to fend off future ridicule, if the story ever got out, but for an instant I wasn't sure I was going to live to tell it! I suddenly had two lungs full of snow that desperately wanted to be full of air, and realized for the first time it could actually be possible to "die laughing," as the saying goes! If I didn't get out of there fast it would definitely be my last laugh. Superman himself would have been proud of me as I dug out of that snow tunnel like a superhero, clawing through the fresh, fluffy flakes until I burst into the fresh, life-giving air, clearing my lungs and gulping for breath. Believe me, there is nothing more terrifying at the age of eight years than being asphyxiated under several feet of snow with a urinating maniac thrashing around beside you.

Growing up is a strange thing. We grow up, or at least convince ourselves that we have, and perhaps go off to college, build a business, raise a family or maybe even take a wrong path and wind up in trouble, and go off to prison. No matter whether our path is good or bad, we spread our wings and leave the old neighborhood behind. We usually plan to come back someday, thinking surely the "neighborhood" will always be there. After a few years, though, anyone who returns to visit their "roots" can tell you it just isn't the same.

When I took my own kids and family back to Crocker many years later, even the few buildings that made up the town as I knew it were mostly gone. Our tiny spot in the universe had gotten even smaller. The old church had vanished, and so had the haunted house. The Voshell place had burned to the ground, and had been replaced by a mobile home. The train track was, for all practical purposes, abandoned. There wasn't much to show my kids. Honestly, I didn't care about any of those buildings being gone, and in truth, I wasn't all that excited about showing them where their dad grew up. Mostly, my thoughts were on the Argetsingers' house. I had gotten word from my parents a few years earlier that Craig had passed away from a massive heart attack, and I was too far away at the time to travel back for his funeral. Now here I was back in Crocker again. I slowed the car a little as we passed by the place. After Homer and Louise had passed away, Craig had moved back in there and it was the last place I saw him alive. I guess I truly came back to honor my childhood friend and say goodbye to him.

My visit to Crocker reminds me of my son Cody's answer to an essay assignment in middle school. He was asked to "Name one thing that no one can take away from you."

His response? "Memories."

Memories. This is what little poverty-stricken Crocker was to me. Crocker held the memory of a time when I shared the wonders of the night sky with a best friend named Craig, when caterpillars and skinned knees were more important than bills and taxes, when 26 kids grew up free and were never, ever lonely. Those days have long since passed by. But the memories are still there, still alive. And that is the sweet side of Crocker, to me.

Sadly, though, my life in Crocker also had a darker side. Not all of the memories from Crocker are ones that cause your heart to smile.

Chapter 6

GROWING UP SCARED

There in front of me, standing in the doorway between the living room and the dining room, was a man ranting in a violent fit of rage. His words came with such force and his gestures were so threatening that I was terrified, frozen in my tracks. Out of fear I wanted to run for my life and yet I feared what he would do to me if I did.

"I ought to take every one of you stupid kids out behind the house, line you up and blow your little heads off. What's wrong with you worthless kids? What were you even thinking? You left a kitchen stool outside under the tree this afternoon! I knew it. Not one of you will ever amount to a damn thing! Not a damn thing! If you ever do anything like that again I'll just go ahead and shoot you, I swear to God, every last one of you..." He gestured with his hand as though sighting us in, and we were speechless.

The man was my father, and I was certain that shooting us, one by one, was exactly what he intended to do someday.

I grew up in a household with an angry father. He himself had suffered much at the hand of his abusive father, who suffered at the hand of the father before him. My dad was not as physically harsh with me as his father was with him; instead, he abused me with verbal and emotional assault. You might say that my dad was a "rage-aholic." If things didn't go just right he came unglued, violently. Something as simple as not being able to find the newspaper when he wanted it could send him into torrents of profanity, banging the furniture, and threatening us within an inch of our lives.

On another occasion my mother had undergone a relatively routine surgery which developed into a something quite non-routine. She had a cardiac arrest on the operating table. For a moment, she was gone. They brought her back, but her condition for several days was immensely critical. We kids visited her in the hospital and she was covered with ice from head to toe. It was so frightening to see my mother in critical condition.

When we returned home, Dad gathered us kids in the kitchen of our big old country home. Then he looked us straight in the eye and said, "You know that this heart attack is you kids' fault, right? You don't behave right; that's why she's had a heart attack. Now you are all going to have to start behaving better so this doesn't happen again." In an instant, the weight of a terrible guilt descended upon me like an avalanche, knocked my feet out from under me, and carried me off in its slimy grip. It was suddenly clear to me, the terrible truth. I was an evil child. My mother's heart attack was my fault. I had caused her to suffer great pain and nearly die. I could hardly breathe. In that moment I realized that I could never truly be a good boy again, because now I had become another kind of a boy – a boy who gave his mother a heart attack. At that moment I decided that I might as well be bad, and I might as well be good at it.

This is the way emotional manipulation works. Emotional manipulation does not help a child learn good behavior; in fact, it does quite the opposite. It backfires. Confusion and a distorted view of self and the world around the child sets in when this type of manipulation is used. As I began to see myself as a hopelessly bad person, I began to live up to that reputation. So I grew up getting into a lot of trouble, though my parents never learned about most of it.

For a long period of time, I hated my father. Resentment and bitterness in my heart turned into an ugly self-devouring monster called rebellion, and undermined my respect for almost all persons in positions of authority, the law included.

In all fairness, my dad's boyhood was pure hell also. His dad was a mean, whiskey-drinking brawler whose favorite pastimes were drinking and fighting. He had a reputation for it around Green County, Iowa. It was often the sole reason he went to town. He would head straight for the bar, belt down a fifth of whiskey and beat somebody half to death. He did not need a reason. He seemed to believe God put other human beings on the planet so he could knock the snot out of them.

Grandpa wasn't just a drunk. He was a mean drunk. He was particularly mean to my dad. There were times, I'm told, when he would come home after a night of drinking, pull my dad out of bed and beat him unconscious. He never showed him any love or acceptance, only disdain with a sting of rejection that lingered and burned hotter than a hornet. My dad himself never heard the things every little boy needs to hear most from his father – "I'm proud of you, son." "Good job, boy!" Or just about every boy's favorite, "Hey, you want to go fishing?"

It grieves me to this day to know that my own father never had a carefree happy childhood. That was stolen from him by the anger and bitterness of my grandfather, whose own childhood had been stolen the same way by his father before him. It is utterly amazing how the same destructive patterns are passed on from generation to generation! I believe, at times, my dad wanted to be a good parent, and when I consider it, he did make my childhood a whole lot better than his own. Even so, as a child, I grew up very afraid of him. It seemed like my dad was a lit fuse ready to ignite into an explosion of anger over just about anything. He was an extremely wounded boy who grew up to be an extremely angry man. Even if he wanted to draw us close, he somehow only managed to push us away.

My mom was ill-equipped to deal with this level of dysfunction. Since her mom was a single mother, and there were 13 siblings in her family of origin, the older ones had to help raise the younger ones. Though her basic needs were met, my mom was raised primarily by older brothers and sisters, which did not fully prepare her for the task of being a wife and mother. Grandma's first husband (my mom's dad), died of tuberculosis after the family had moved to California in hope of a "cure." Grandma then remarried, but husband number two had the unfortunate trait of beating her up at times. One day when one of her older sons came home from hunting, he found his stepfather beating up his mom. This son sighted husband number two in the crosshairs of his hunting gun scope, pulled the trigger, and dropped him dead at her feet. No charges were filed. Grandma remained single for a season after that, then attempted marriage once more and took husband number three. The third man was the meanest yet. He told his kids, "When I die, I want you to bury me face down so that the whole world can kiss my ass." Grandma eventually threw this joker out, and after that decided she was better off on her own. But she was far from alone, not with 13 kids to raise.

She was harangued by her family to farm out some of these kids to other homes for raising. But Theo May Shackelford, as she was known, set her jaw and stubbornly determined to raise each and every one of her own children, with or without the help of anyone else. To do this she worked a fulltime job and also ran a small farm. Theo May Shackelford is one of the top three people I have come to admire most in my family. She raised her entire large brood out of sheer grit and determination.

Still, the absence of a mother in the home took its toll on my mom. She grew up not really knowing what it was to be given the love and individual attention so vital to nurturing healthy children. Missing also was the day-to-day practical demonstration of mothering and running a household, the kind a little girl observes over a lifetime, so vital to passing on these feminine skills. So it was tough for Raetta Kopaska, who also married an angry man, to step into the roles of "wife and mother" and hold things together.

Home life in Crocker was what it was; not too pretty, not too much chance of change. There was a sizable amount of confusion and pain mingled in with those happier memories of childhood friends and the great outdoors. Alcohol, anger, and abuse were an unholy trinity – a three-headed dragon that terrorized our family tree and attempted to pass itself down into yet another generation. But this time, something different happened. Someone intervened. Better seeds were sown, and it happened in Polk City, Iowa.

Polk City was one of those small Iowa communities with a park right in the center of town, complete with a large white gazebo and an old cannon facing Main Street. This was the place where once a year one of the greatest spectacles on the planet Earth took place – Polk City Days. About the first Saturday in September, the townspeople and all the people of the surrounding communities came out to celebrate. It was a small town carnival at its best. What a time it was for us kids! The sound and smells of buttery popcorn bursting into puffy delights, the scent of barbecued pork that was always slow cooked in a big pit, dug in the ground, and of course the all-time trial of human endurance and raw courage – the Greased Pig Contest.

I can't imagine what it must feel like for a pig to have its body smeared with grease only to be thrown into the middle of a bunch of swine-crazed children, whooping and hollering, dancing and diving, risking all for the glory of being the one to catch the terrified creature and toss him into the holding pen, and winning the Grand Prize. I can't imagine, nor do I really want to. All I know is that back then, the Grand Prize, probably a bag of candy or five bucks that would immediately be spent on a bag of candy, was worth it all -- the grease, the dirt, the 150 flailing elbows, hands and knees. I never won the grand prize, so I am not sure what they gave away. With my luck, it would have been the pig itself, which would have only meant more chores for me.

At any rate, it was late one evening after a Polk City Days celebration, after I once again failed to catch the greased pig, when an unexpected event took place which set a different course for my life. I was only eight or nine at the time, and was playing with my brothers and sisters and some other kids in the park. My parents went across the street to Mary's Bar to have a couple of drinks with some friends. Rural Iowa towns were safe after dark in those days; there was a sense of community where people looked out for each other and each other's kids. My parents didn't drink much, but when they did, they knew better than to bring their kids in a bar. They showed us where they would be, right across the street, and gave us strict orders to stay and play only in the park, within view.

We played until we were hot and sweaty, and then sat down to rest on the curb facing Polk City's Main Street. I don't know where they came from, but a group of teenagers descended on us from somewhere out of the dark reaches of the park. One of them sat down with me in front of the old cannon, with its long silvery barrel pointing straight ahead. He began a conversation of some urgency, the contents of which left me about as soon as I heard him say it, and then we prayed together. The only thing I remember was one question he asked after that prayer. Even as a little boy of eight or nine, I knew it was a profound question. In fact, it was a question that has stayed with me for the rest of my life.

"Kc, do you know that since you prayed that prayer with me, if you walked out into the street tonight and got run over by a car, you would spend the rest of eternity in heaven with Jesus?" he asked.

His question puzzled me. I could not grasp what it meant. Yet, somewhere deep inside my little boy's mind, I sensed that something very, very important had just taken place. Without fully understanding what I had done, I had asked Jesus Christ to come into my heart and life and save me from my sins.

Even though I never saw that teenage boy again, I believe that it was that prayer together in the Polk City Park that evening that set a different course for my future. I never knew the boy's name, or what church he attended, but today I wish I could thank him. Because there was no follow-up to complete what was begun in my life that night, it took many, many more years after that prayer of commitment before I actually understood what it meant to be a follower of Jesus Christ. Nevertheless, one of the Savior's promises was initiated – I had given my life to Jesus, and He would be faithful to me, even if I was not faithful to Him, because He refuses to disown His children. (II Timothy 2:13)

Something new, a seed of a better future, had been planted in my life that night. It was a tiny seed, but the seed had the power to grow up and transform my life. One day that seed would grow into something bigger and stronger than the three-headed dragon of "Alcohol, Abuse and Anger" in my family tree. Something big and strong enough, in fact, to slay the dragon, when the time was right.

Chapter 7

HELL IN A CUBE

From the hospital in Florence, Colorado, Floyd and I were transferred to the airport in Pueblo where we were picked up by a medical transport jet. In a strange sort of way, I was excited about riding in a jet for the first time in my life. I remained conscious and cognizant of everything going on around me during the entire flight to San Antonio. The circumstances weren't too agreeable, though; inside the jet I was completely packed in ice except for my face. This was done for the purpose of controlling swelling and reducing further tissue damage. I do not think this procedure of ice immersion is current, standard protocol. All that I know is that all of that ice was cold enough to give a penguin goose bumps. I went from being nearly burned to death to freezing to death in the same day. On top of this, I was ravenously thirsty but could not ingest liquids. I could, however, nibble on – you guessed it – more ice. I am pretty sure that by the time I landed in San Antonio, between being packed in a life size cooler and nibbling on ice, I was peeing ice cubes. You know you're having a bad day when you go from being a flaming soufflé to a Popsicle all within a twenty-four hour period.

Seated near me in the plane was my sister Carol, who was chosen to ride along. I recall the worried look on her face, but no conversation. I also recall that I had never been so thirsty in all of my life. I spent most of the flight begging the attending physician for more ice chips. My burn injuries caused my capillaries to essentially leak, causing life threatening electrolyte imbalance and the marked swelling that forced Dr. Berge to perform the deep incisions on my arms and torso. Had he not done that, the swelling would have restricted blood flow, causing further complications. Fluids had built up so fast in my body that I soon developed hyponatremia, that is, the sodium levels in my blood dropped precipitously, impeding the water levels in and around my cells, thus fueling my extreme thirst. Athletes have died from this same condition. The combination of rapid body fluid loss and only re-hydrating with water leaches sodium and other minerals out of their body, bringing it to the point of death. This was the scenario setting up in my body, becoming more severe by the minute. Death was hot on my heels.

Shortly before arriving at the base in San Antonio I lost consciousness. I don't recall the landing or being taken off of the plane and loaded onto a medical transport bus, but at this point every step of the journey was a harrowing race against time. Even on the transport bus, we barely missed catastrophe, when it was discovered that there were not enough filled oxygen bottles on board to keep me supplied with life-sustaining O_2 during the short journey from the landing strip to the hospital proper. One of my lungs had burn injuries, my heart was under significant stress, and fluid imbalances were impeding my breathing. Insufficient available oxygen at this point was no small matter. I do recall, though, briefly waking up on the bus and taking a blurry look around. I could hardly focus, mentally or visually, and could hear nothing. Quickly, I retreated back into unconsciousness.

When I finally began to regain some sense of awareness, I was in a bizarre world of strange sights and intense pain. None of it made sense to me. I didn't remember where I was. I seemed to be crawling through a strange, tubular maze made of a semi-transparent substance with undulating colors. I perceived the colors to be flames, but they did not behave like flames of a typical fire. The translucent colors of the flames danced and flowed as though a strange current drew them along faster than I could crawl past them. They caused the pain I was in and in my hallucinogenic state I kept trying to crawl past them to the end of the tunnel where I knew I would find relief. In my drugged, traumatized mind the flaming tunnel represented the blistering, searing pain that was utterly torturing me. Somehow, though, I couldn't find my way out; I was a tormented soul. I was in hell.

From that first hellish nightmare I transitioned into another equally bizarre hallucination. In this one, an unidentifiable person held me face down while Virgil flogged my face and torso with a long, curling whip made out of barbed wire that looked like a grotesquely exaggerated jigsaw blade. Again, this hallucination represented extreme pain and my inability to escape it. Since I had no time reference whatsoever, I can't say how long these hallucinations lasted or at what point they started. It seemed like they lasted forever. They simply would not let go of me.

After the first series of hallucinations finally ended, I recall awakening with very poor eyesight. What I could see was blurry at best and I had virtually no peripheral vision. I could tell that I was in a bed with railings on both sides, but I still did not know where I was. There were tubes and wires attached all over me. Only one thought was running through my mind – escape. I must have been in the burn center for only a short while, since my upper body was still swollen to about twice its normal size.

I started flopping around until I was able to turn sideways in the bed. Somehow I managed to launch the lower half of my body over the left-side railing at which point I began rocking back and forth until I was actually able to hurl myself over the rail landing on my feet. When I touched down, I was facing a door to a hallway where I could barely make out a person sitting at a desk. I heard some clattering, probably I.V. poles and other contraptions tipping over, the orderly screaming, and then through my blurry vision saw him running toward me. I passed out before he reached me. I never was one for lying around much.

Eventually, the information about where I was took hold in my mind, as well as my recollection of the accident. I was in the burn center at Brooke Army Hospital first level of intensive care, an alien place known in the hospital as "The Cube." During the period of time I was there, it was partitioned off into eight or so sections divided by sliding curtains, forming separate cubicles, thus the name "Cube." It was designed in such a way that it could be quickly reconfigured to accommodate many more beds in case of a military skirmish or a natural disaster of catastrophic proportions. All the burn victims had another name for it, though. To us, it was just known as "Hell."

My parents were notified, somewhere in this course of events, that they should get to San Antonio as soon as possible, but not to expect to see me alive.

When they arrived, the on-call doctor led them to my bed, the first one just inside the door of the Cube. Both my mother and father would have walked right on past without recognizing me if the doctor had not stopped at the foot of my bed. My father later told of how he wondered why the doctor stopped at that bed. Even looking straight at me, he had no recognition at all that the poor soul lying there was his own son. Instead, he only felt pity for the poor dying person in that bed, swollen and burned beyond recognition. When the doctor told my parents directly that this was indeed their own son, my mother blacked out, straight away. In fact, my mother blacked out several times in the early days of my treatment, until she could get used to looking at my swollen, burned body with inch-wide incisions running the length of my arms.

The Cube was hot. It was permeated with the stench of burned and infected flesh. The moans and screams of tormented burn victims never ended. Death and dying were our constant companions. The Cube functioned at Brooke Hospital as an intensive care unit within an intensive care unit. The other one was located above on the second floor. Due to infections and a whole host of other burn-related complications, people still died after "graduating" from the Cube to the second floor. The second floor intensive care was, however, revered almost as a hallowed and mystical place by the burn victims in the Cube. It was there that most of the skin grafting took place, as well as any physical therapy and other procedures aimed at healing. More important, it represented a major milestone of survival, and the beginning of regaining freedom and preparing to go home.

In the Cube, though, the primary goal was just to stay alive. A lot of people left the Cube in body bags, something to which I never grew accustomed. All of us there were fighting the same struggle for life, and when one lost that struggle, it felt as though a part of the rest of us died with them.

The temperature was kept at about one hundred degrees because charred skin loses its ability to retain body heat. Even with such a high temperature, I constantly asked for a heat lamp to be stationed by my bed. It was a luxurious accommodation for my constantly chilled body but was available for limited usage. Heat lamps contributed to dehydration and had to be used sparingly. My burned skin was constantly oozing fluids. I couldn't afford anything that exacerbated the problem. It was a crazy existence to be in constant pain from third degree burns, while at the same time feeling as if I was freezing to death.

Life in the Cube was an endless eternity of unquenchable torment. Every day was framed by pain, pain like no other. Pain of this caliber causes minutes to seem like hours, hours like days, and days to blend together into a sea of torture. I was thirsty 24 hours a day; parched dry, always. I couldn't drink water my first couple of months in the hospital. Because my body was burning calories faster than they could be replaced, every ounce of food and liquid had to supply nutrients in order to keep me alive. No regular water was allowed, only liquid with nutrients. How I longed for just one long, cool refreshing drink of water!

I hated the Cube. It was a nightmarish place of pain and confusion. The confusion was caused by a combination of the hallucinations, pain medication, and not understanding what other people were doing to me. Intense hallucinations set in, not only from the drugs, but also from my brain's own defense mechanisms against the pain and trauma. There were extended periods of time when I was completely disoriented and out of touch with reality. Snakes and dinosaur-like creatures crawled across the ceiling and my bed. I was afraid that when I got up and put my feet on the floor, small, brown haired creatures with sharp teeth would bite me and give me rabies. Sometimes I hallucinated that I was at parties, and other times that I was fighting Germans. I was afraid that the Germans were sneaking into the hospital and poisoning my food.

I often thought I was fighting World War II era German soldiers. Don't ask me why I thought that Germans were out to get me. I am one. In one incident I was flowing in and out of reality when a nurse placed a tray of food in front me and then walked away. I was propped up in a wheelchair that was set up with a table-like device so that my food could be placed in front of me and someone could sit next to it and feed me. As I sat there with the food in front of me, I watched a German soldier sneak out of a closet, pour his vial of poison in my food and then vanish.

"Ha! I caught him! And he thought he got away with it!" I thought, "Well, I'll show him!" Quick as lightening, I defiantly swept my arm across the table, caught the tray, and knocked it all to the floor with a loud clatter.

My proud moment of victory was short lived. Post haste, an extremely agitated nurse was in my face yelling at me for my bad behavior, and that German soldier was nowhere to be found. I don't remember a word she said, but it upset me terribly. Why was I the one in trouble? I didn't know what I was doing; it was those damn Germans.

Some of the most troublesome hallucinations were the ones involving flies. I thought they were landing on my skin and giving me infections or laying eggs, which hatched into maggots. I constantly asked orderlies to kill them for me, which some actually pretended to do. I hated the flies the most.

Hallucinations caused a lot of strange behaviors, most of which are laughable in hindsight. But I do recall one incident from my first few days at Brooke that I truly regret. My parents were in the room trying to communicate to me when a female orderly came in. By this time I had lost my eyesight altogether. I remember her walking up to my bed, but I could not discern what she was saying or doing. I assumed that she was another German soldier out to get me. My legs still had a good deal of strength in them, so I bent one up and kicked hard in the direction of her voice. Unfortunately I hit my target right in the sternum. She went flying, and I could hear a lot of loud clattering. I was immediately reprimanded for what I had done. Though I could not see the damage I had caused her, I was told that I had badly bruised her sternum. As a first responder for a local fire department today, I am surprised I did not break her sternum along with disconnecting some of her ribs. When I came back to my senses and realized what I had done, I felt sorry for her. I don't think she held the same sentiment toward me.

I was on a water-free diet, which I hated, but it did have one advantage – in order to increase the calories in my diet, I was allowed a beer quota, two cans a day. As I began to adjust to the constant pain and the hallucinations subsided, my devious brain began scheming ways that I could "stretch" that two-can quota into four. I was allowed to have my beers one right after the other, if I chose. So one day I got a bright idea – I could use staff shift changes to increase my consumption. I waited until near the end of an afternoon shift to ask for my two beers and drank them fast before the new shift came on, so that someone would carry off the empties. When the shift change was complete, I immediately asked for two more beers, which I was given. Success! Evidently, beer consumption records were not well kept.

Unfortunately, I did not take into consideration the medication schedule. After drinking the two additional beers, it was also time for an injection of pain medication.

Soon after administering the medicine, I passed out cold. When I finally came too, I was berated up one side and down the other. Some of the scolding included colorful versions of "You could have died pulling a stunt like that." Not only did I get a lot of people in trouble, but far worse, I lost my beer privileges. I was not a very popular patient after that, either. Somehow, I still managed to get some alcohol snuck in from time-to-time, though. I was a fool, determined to engage in a pattern of self-destructive behavior even at a time when I was fighting for my life.

The Cube was Brooke Army Hospital's battleground for life, and every day there were casualties. One day a young, expectant mother would be wailing in agony and grief over her just-deceased husband. Another day it would be a soldier's wife. Often the word solemnly passed among us that yet another fellow patient had fallen. The saddest deaths of all were the lonely ones, the ones where it appeared there was no one in the deceased person's life who cared enough to be there when they died. It was as though they came into the world unknown and left the same way. It was odd to be conversing about future plans with the person across the room from me one day, and then the next day find out they were gone forever. I had no fear of dying, and did not analyze it much. Death seemed to me just another version of the pain that had become such a big a part of my world. I often wondered myself if I would survive the Cube. Sometimes there seemed to be no light at the end of the tunnel.

When we lost sight of the light at the end of the tunnel, however, the light seemed to come and find us. Once I was infected with a fast-acting organism that was unresponsive to antibiotics. A "bug" had settled in my heart and was destroying it, particularly one heart valve. The resident doctor told my mother that I would probably not make it through the night and that she should begin to make funeral arrangements immediately. After he walked out of my cubicle, she sat quietly by my bed wrestling with God in prayer. Finally she stood up, turned around to walk out of the room and in the process threw up her hands and simply said out loud, "I can't do this anymore." As soon as the words came out of her mouth, she was flooded with "a peace that was beyond my understanding," as she later recalled. Whether she knew it or not, she was quoting a portion of Scripture found in Philippians 4:7, "And the peace of God, which transcends all understanding, will guard your hearts and your minds in Christ Jesus." (NIV) That night, she went back to her dormitory, and instead of making funeral arrangements, she lay down, fell asleep, and had the most restful night since the whole ordeal started. The mysterious infection healed miraculously, and I survived.

Sadly, it was Floyd who did not survive. I never found out exactly how long Floyd lived after the accident because the information was withheld from me for a time. But when I was eventually told that he hadn't made it, the news of Floyd's death hit me with a deep, gut-wrenching grief. I had only known him for part of one day, yet his passing felt like I was losing a long-time friend. Together, we had experienced an extraordinary trauma, which created an instant bond. News of his death profoundly affected me. It was one of the rare moments that I cried at Brooke.

After leaving the burn center I was haunted by a recurring hallucination from the Cube. In it, a man moaned in anguish from intolerable pain, while nurses were yelling, and a doctor kept telling them to shut up and keep cutting. It was a gruesome dream of an amputation being performed without the aid of anesthetic. Gut-wrenching and bloody, its graphic images of a man crying out, while his legs were cut off right in front of me, reappeared over and over in my consciousness. These mental images troubled me enough that I confided in my mother about the hallucination, and asked if she knew why this scene might haunt me so. She did. The hallucination would not leave my subconscious because it was not a hallucination at all; it was an actual memory. An emergency surgery had been performed in front of me in the Cube while I was in a deeply medicated state, assumed by the medical staff to be unconscious. It is troubling to lose the ability to distinguish between fact and fiction in these memories, but when reality is this horrific, losing that ability may be a strange mercy, after all.

That was life in the Cube. People came, people went, many lived; most died. No one in the Cube was guaranteed anything but unmitigated pain, a chance to fight for their lives, and difficult choices. The most critical choice in the Cube, perhaps the only real choice any patient had, was the choice to keep on fighting for his life, or quit trying. Regardless, the Cube was, in many ways, just one long nightmare. When gangrene attacked my hands and the surgeons wanted to do full scale amputations and completely remove both hands and most of my arms , however, the doctors at Brooke came face to face with another kind of nightmare: the fury of my father, Jack Kopaska.

Chapter 8

SKINNED ALIVE

"HELL, NO! I AM NOT signing those papers!"
"But Mr. Kopaska…"

"That boy would be better off dead! You're NOT cuttin' off his arms, his hands, or nothing else!"

"Mr. Kopaska, we can't save his life without the amputations. There are excellent prosthetic limbs, and we can leave enough of his arm so he can be fitted with a prosthetic arm and hand… He's young, he'll learn to use them. But if we don't get rid of that gangrene, he's going to die."

"LET HIM DIE! You hear me? Just let him die! He'd be better off dead than living like that. What kind of a life is that? NO!! I'm *not signing.*"

Brooke's head surgeon threw his hands up and stormed out, then removed himself completely from my case. I had survived the initial shock of the burn, but in less than three short weeks of the accident, gangrene was setting into my badly burned hands. The only safe medical path was to amputate my left arm at the shoulder, my right arm at the elbow, and anything else endangered.

Because of my dad's obstinacy, a Japanese surgeon practicing in the hospital stepped into the case. He finally agreed to do exploratory surgery and see if there was any possible alternative to wholesale amputation. Good thing he wasn't a German.

After exploratory surgery, looking for some hope that my hands were at least somewhat salvageable, the new surgeon decided wholesale amputation of my hands and arms was not necessary after all. They could keep both of my arms and save some of the hands. My fingers were cut away above the second digit on both hands, and I kept most of my left thumb, but the right thumb was lost.

As the anesthesia began to wear off and my eyes slowly came into focus, the first thing I noticed was the white gauze wrapped around both of my hands. I knew. Nobody had to tell me. My fingers were gone. I am sure I was told ahead of time that they would be amputated, but in my constant delirium it did not register in my mind. This was the second time I cried at Brooke. Through the tears, I asked, "Why my fingers? Why did they have to take my fingers? What about playing the bass? How am I ever going to play the bass again?" It had been my dream to attend a music college in Chicago. I knew I was a good musician, maybe even good enough to go "pro." Now, like a broken guitar string, my fingers could no longer create music. Living was getting harder to do.

It is one thing to see another man's blood run, but it is something else when it is your own. Every day after that surgery the bandages on what remained of my hands had to be changed. After a bath or shower they would be unwrapped. If I left my hands down, dangling by my side, the blood would run out, big drop after big drop. The orderly caring for me at the time would bark out a command for me to lift my hands up so the bleeding would not be so profuse.

Somewhere in the midst of recovery, I even went completely blind for an extended time and lost my voice as well. My blindness was so complete that one day, while I was sitting up in a wheelchair with my mother nearby, a doctor attempted to determine the extent of it using a very simple, basic test.

"Kc, I am going to shine a flashlight in your eyes and I want you to tell me if you see any light." I could see nothing, but judging by the direction of his voice, I looked toward where I thought the light beam should be.

My world was totally black. "I don't see anything," I said.

The doctor was grimly silent for a few moments. "Mrs. Kopaska, your son's eyesight appears to be gone and I don't know how much sight he will ever recover," he said. "I can give you no promises that he will recover any of it, ever." With that, he put up his flashlight and walked out of the room.

Though his hopeless announcement should have torn me apart emotionally, I really wasn't upset; in fact, I did not feel much of anything at all. The only reason that I can think of for this is that when God said to me in the field that day, "Everything is going to be all right," His promise planted itself so deeply in my soul that hope simply would not let go of me.

From that point on, the only thing that was done to treat my eyes was that several times a day someone would squirt salve into them. I suppose it was an antibiotic ointment applied in order to reduce the risk of infection. According to my recollection, there were no surgeries or other procedures performed to try and save my eyesight. Somehow, in the end, however, I walked out of the hospital with 20/20 vision. It was another miracle; one of many. My case continued to defy medical explanation.

On several occasions my life was endangered by various infections. The body's main defense mechanism against dangerous micro-organisms is the skin. I had lost 60 percent of that shield. At one point three other men and I contracted the same bacterial infection on the same day. The other three men died, I lived. For some reason, I kept dodging all the bullets in what seemed like a burn center version of Russian Roulette. At Brooke, every day was like a spin of a revolver's cylinder with five empty chambers but the sixth loaded with a bullet. Just to wake up in the morning felt like pointing the gun at my head. It was impossible to know which day might fire that fatal shot. But somehow for me, death's trigger just kept clicking on the empty chambers, day after day.

In order for my deteriorating health to stabilize, regain the ability to ward off infections, and have any hope for survival, the doctors began the tedious work of replacing my dead, burned skin with grafted living skin tissue taken from the few good spots left on my body. This was done in roughly two processes. The first process, called debridement, involved a number of procedures that were used to remove dead tissue. Though there were many procedures, they all amounted to the same thing – relentless pain. At times, tissue was simply snipped off with a pair of scissors, as in the case of my ears. My right one is completely gone, but that does not mean someone walked in the room one day and simply lopped it off. As it became apparent that a portion of ear tissue was not going to regenerate, an orderly would snip it off with a pair of surgical scissors. Oddly enough, this was the only debriding that did not hurt.

Another debriding procedure consisted of having moistened gauze laid across my entire back in a thick layer where it would soon begin to wick up the fluids oozing out of open areas. These excretions would dry and adhere to the gauze like a very tenacious adhesive. The next day I would be told to straddle a chair backwards and hold tightly onto it. The whole thickness of the gauze would then be slowly peeled off, tearing loose dead tissue and other matter. I don't know how long it took to complete the process, but it seemed like it would never end. After the gauze was completely removed, I would be given a bath and then new gauze would be reapplied.

The most dreadful form of debridement, by far, was being "tanked." This consisted of being placed on a stretcher and lowered into a stainless steel tank, more specifically a Hubbard Tank, where orderlies would commence to cutting off dead skin with scalpels and scissors. The Hubbard Tank was a whirlpool roughly configured in the shape of an hour glass. The circulating water helped rinse away blood and debrided tissue. The first time that I was tanked, I was given a shot of morphine but told that the shot would have no effect in deadening any pain I was about to experience. It was administered for the sole purpose of helping me calm down once the procedure was over. They were right. The morphine did not lessen the pain one bit.

"I don't want to hear you yell, scream or cuss. You just lay there and take it," I was told by an orderly just before my first tanking.

Having no idea what was to come, I just silently looked up at him.

Lying there in that cold walled, stainless steel tank, I could feel every slice of the scalpel and every snip of the scissors. I was literally being skinned alive. Every layer of dead skin had to be removed in order to expose viable, nerve-laden tissue that could receive fresh skin grafts. On several occasions, a large vein was nicked and blood spurted out with such force it shot over the side of the tank. A surgeon was called into the room in order to sew up the bleeder, and then the cutting continued. Unimaginable torture had only just begun.

I was tanked twice a day for two weeks. It was the only way that doctors could better control the infections that were wracking my body and threatening my life. To this day I am at a loss for words to adequately describe the inconceivable torture of the tank. It is probably a good thing. Being systematically skinned alive took me to the very edge of insanity. For some of my fellow patients, it took them over that edge for a time. It finally took me over, too.

During my season of being tanked, I coincidentally contracted a staph infection that caused huge boils to break out on what good skin I had left. After debriding me, those attending to me would switch to scraping the boils. This hurt so badly, almost as badly as being skinned. Eventually, my mind attempted to create an escape route from the pain. I began to mentally regress back to the stage of infancy. As strange as that may sound, I actually remember the experience, though vaguely. I lost my ability to speak and began to babble like a baby. I was incapable of any complex cognitive abilities and even if I could have fed myself, I would not have remembered how. I did not understand what people said to me. I saw shapes and faces in abstract form. I don't know how long I was in this state of being, nor am I sure at what point during my time spent in the Cube that this happened.

One day, as I was enduring an extremely painful procedure, an older hospital chaplain happened to be present. He told me that there was a way to use my mind to at least temporarily escape some of the pain.

"I am going to rub your temples, and as I do I want you to close your eyes and in your mind focus real hard on places or things that make you feel good."

I closed my eyes and pictured in my mind my favorite places back home such as the beach at Saylorville Lake where I partied and swam with my friends. Incredibly, the pain began to fade. As I became more adept at creating mental images of home, short lived as they were, I actually experienced significant relief from the pain, even while in the tank. When the nurses and orderlies would start the procedures, I simply "left" on mental excursions to all my favorite places. I visited Big Creek Lake. I gazed over the vast, lush corn and bean fields of Iowa, and I traipsed through the hardwood forests on imaginary hunting and camping trips. It worked.

Soon, visiting these places in my mind created a longing in me to be in the out-of-doors again. As a young boy, it seemed more familiar and natural to me to be outside rather than in a building. I grew up in the country and the "Great Outdoors" was always just a few steps off my back porch. It was not unusual for my friends and me to play outside, all day, in good or bad weather, from the time we got up until the time we went to bed. The outdoor world was, to us, a fun place for discovery and exploration. It was in the tank, oddly enough, that I realized that while I had been playing as a child, something else had been happening. The Great Outdoors had quietly taken root in my soul, and now it lived inside of me, like an old friend waiting to be rediscovered. Even the pain of the tank could not take that Great Outdoors away. In fact, visits to the tank quickly became my only hope to visit with this dear old friend.

There was a small window that folded inward in the tank room. I spotted it during my first trip there. After each brutal 20 to 30 minute session of debridement was over, I would beg the orderlies attending to me to open that little window and lift me up to it, close enough so that I could get a whiff of fresh air and a glimpse of green grass and blue sky. From the window, I could also see part of a tree with its leaves fluttering in the breeze. I was never a "tree hugger" but in those few moments by the window, I embraced what the Great Outdoors meant to me – Life. That window became my umbilical cord to the light of life and rationality, saving me from the insanity and darkness brought on by debridement.

Today, life still has its painful moments and when they come, I do exactly what I did in the tank. I focus my attention on home, though not a home found in this world. Instead, I try to imagine my eternal home where, according to the Bible in Revelation 21:3-4, there will be no more pain or suffering. In that home there will be neither death, nor dying, nor mourning, nor crying. It is a place where God will walk among His people and wipe every tear from their eyes. I hope to take a lot of people with me when I go there to live forever.

Chapter 9

THE SECOND FLOOR

When I got news that I was finally graduating to the "hallowed" second floor of the burn center, I was elated. This was not a guarantee of survival, however. There were still things that could go wrong such as infections and complications during surgery, but those concerns never crossed my mind at the time. I was too preoccupied with once again being able to drink all of the good old cool, clear water that I wanted. On the hallowed second floor I had a radio by my bed and a TV on the wall in front of my bed, two luxuries that reminded me of a lost civilization I once belonged to and desperately wanted to find again.

By the time I settled into my new accommodations, most, if not all, of my third degree burned flesh had been debrided. Now, it was time for the doctors to begin peeling off good skin so that it could be grafted onto areas where I no longer had any. Such a large area of my body needed skin grafts that the process had to be done in stages. It wasn't fun. Typically the process started with one or two blood transfusions the day before the surgery. The blood gave my body strength to endure the skin grafting ordeal; unfortunately it also gave me something else. A tainted batch of blood deposited a hidden enemy in my system which would not be discovered for years to come; discovered not only much later, but as it turned out, just in the nick of time.

Meanwhile, in the operating room used for skin grafting, the harvesting procedure would begin with marking off an area of good skin on one of my legs, then injecting water under the first two layers of skin at the donor site. The raised skin would then be removed with a device called a Dermatome. After removal, another device poked it full of holes so that it could be stretched out before being sewn onto the graft site. This procedure allowed donor skin to go farther, a very important factor since donor sites could only be harvested three times before they built up too much scar tissue themselves to be of any use.

Obviously, skin suitable for grafting was truly priceless and in limited supply. When skin was taken from a donor site, doctors often took a little more than they needed in order to patch open areas where part of a graft did not take or for later, less invasive surgeries. Even in high level medical facilities, human error invades, however. At the time, this "extra skin" was kept in a medium inside of a refrigerator – the same refrigerator where the orderlies kept their cold drinks and lunches. One day, an orderly did not get the door closed all of the way and all of the extra skin, from myself and other patients, was ruined and had to be discarded. The orderlies caught a lot of grief from all of us over that. We didn't let them forget this easily.

Lying on a conventional bed to recover was out of the question after skin grafts. When grafts were done on my torso, I could no longer lie on a regular hospital bed, but instead was placed in a contraption called an air-fluidized bed. I hated the thing, especially when I had to lie face down, and called the thing a lot of other names, none of which are found in Webster's Collegiate Dictionary. It consisted of an air-permeable mattress that was filled with millions of tiny silicone beads. The air-fluidized bed was invented in order to alleviate any pressure points on the body. It really did feel like floating on air. I had to be placed on the air bed lying on the opposite side of a new graft. Lying on the graft would have prevented it from taking, so if the surgery was performed on my back I had to lie on my stomach and vice versa. Lying on a conventional bed in the same position, for extended periods of time, would have caused nasty bedsores on my fragile skin. The air bed had its own dangers though, suffocation being one possibility. In order to keep my face from being buried in the air-fluidized beads, a food tray was placed on it in the location of my head and then pressed down into the mattress by two poles that extended to the ceiling. I was always afraid one of those poles was going to slip, and I would not be able to yell for help. After every back surgery, I had to lie on the bed, face down, with only the tray to look at. The only way I could eat at those times was to be hand fed. I resented having my newfound freedom on the second floor taken away again by skin grafting surgeries. I don't know any better way to express my feelings toward the air bed when lying face down on it except to say that the whole experience just sucked.

Finally, I was through this process and healed enough to have visitors again. My brother and sister and an old friend came to visit me at the burn center.

"What can we do for you Kc?" they joked. "Besides get you a beer?"

"I just want to go outside," I said. "See if there is any way you can take me outside." I wanted so badly to be able to look at trees and grass and flowers, and once again smell a fresh breeze and hear the birds sing. After several days of requesting permission, I was given the "OK" for my first excursion outside since being admitted to the hospital. I was still too weak to walk and had too many open wounds to allow my body contact with the elements, so I was placed in a wheelchair, completely covered with a sheet except for my head, and sent out the door in their care.

Behind the hospital was a garden area that Mamie Eisenhower had built for the hospital. A concrete pool, which had not been used for some time, was located in the middle of the garden. This pool was designed to be deep enough to be used for physical therapy exercise for the patients. A sidewalk wound around the pool through trees and shrubs. I asked my brother John to take me for a stroll around the garden. It felt as though I was traveling through the most beautiful garden in the entire world. Trees were vividly green and the flowers exploded with color, as bright as any I had ever seen before. The sound of chirping birds seemed like a symphony of sweet, soothing melodies. I felt like a little child on his first excursion into the forest. I could not take all of this beauty in at once, it was almost overwhelming. The sidewalk seemed to wind around for the longest time. If someone would have told me about God at that moment in the Mamie Eisenhower Garden, I am sure I would have instantly fallen in love with Him for creating something so beautiful.

During a trip through San Antonio 15 years later, I revisited the Mamie Eisenhower Garden and was amazed at what I saw. It really wasn't a very large area. Most of the shrubs had been removed and the pool was now filled in with dirt, although you could clearly see its outline. I thought to myself that perhaps this garden area hadn't been as spectacular as it seemed when I observed it for the first time from that wheelchair. Perhaps I just appreciated it so much, along with all of the things that I had always taken for granted. On this visit, the garden's trees seemed once again normal, just regular old trees. The only "symphonic birds" around that day were sparrows and starlings – neither one known for having much of a voice. Still, the Mamie Eisenhower Garden was the place where I physically connected with my old friend, the Great Outdoors, and walking through it again, 15 years later, was deeply moving to me, especially since this time I was sober enough to actually enjoy it.

Toward the end of my hospitalization, patients who were progressing were allowed to spend time in a room with floor-to-ceiling windows and an extraordinary view. I went there every morning, and periodically I would walk to the room at other times throughout the day when it was empty and gaze out one of the windows. I would watch everything from the pigeons that landed on the stoop to rest and coo, to the many activities occurring on the expansive military parade ground outside. There were dress rehearsals, choppers landing and taking off, and military personnel doing all kinds of other things. For a short while I would forget where I was and get lost in the green grass, blue skies and warm sunlight streaming in through those tall windows. It all added to my growing homesickness. I began to long for home.

One morning, about the end of August, I had a little time to walk down to the window room before breakfast and the dressing change. Gazing at an early salmon-colored Texas sunrise, I suddenly became desperately homesick. An overwhelming yearning for all that was familiar rose up in me.

"I want to go home," raced through my thoughts, but it was more than a thought. It was a sharp edged desire, an unexpected stab of nearly unbearable pain deep inside.

As I stood in front of that window, watching the salmon sky intensify to a brilliant red Texas sunrise, I realized I was facing east, more or less the direction of Iowa. It felt like years, not months, since I had been there. Home, where tall green cornfields stretched from horizon to horizon; home, with its hot muggy summers and cold snowy winters; home, with its fishing in Big Creek Lake or hunting in oak and hickory woodlands with friends; home, to familiar faces and family.

Yes, I was ready to go home. Past ready. The yearning of my soul formed itself into tears that welled up in my eyes, slid down my badly scarred face and became a silent prayer. I began to weep. God saw my tears, and heard my cry.

This is the third time I can recall crying at Brooke. Strangely, I had no sense of feeling sorry for myself there, and intense pain became so commonplace that it was hardly worth crying about. Perhaps the absence of self-pity was the result of being surrounded by so many others who were in similar straits. Besides, if any of us were free enough from pain to complain about it, we did not want to waste the energy doing so. There was life to think about. We all knew too many former patients who no longer had the "blessing" of feeling pain. Feeling pain meant that we were at least still alive.

But there I was, tears streaming down my face in front of the east-facing window. God was active in my life then, though I did not recognize it at the time. I felt so alone. Today, it is easy for me to imagine that I actually was not alone, that Jesus was standing there beside me, with His arm around my shoulder, simply saying, "I know." And He did know. No other human being has known homesickness as acutely as He did when he walked this world. His home had been in the perfect, loving presence of God in heaven, but

He voluntarily left there in order to traipse around on this decaying planet. For a time, He relinquished his prestige as the King of Kings, and became "homeless" on this earth. Yes, Jesus understood how I felt.

Little did I know that God was busy behind the scenes answering this cry of my heart. It was not long after that lonesome, momentary vigil that the head surgeon of Brooke gave me a bedside visit. For several minutes the doctor, who was one of the greatest burn treatment pioneers alive, stood by my bed, looking down at me with a puzzled expression and scratching his head. His hesitance began to really annoy me, and I was just about to let him know it, when he stopped me in my tracks and rocked my world.

"I don't know why, but you are going home in two weeks," the doctor said tersely. With that, he turned around and walked down the hall, leaving me stunned.

Suddenly and unexpectedly, "going home" was just around the corner.

Kopaska family before Accident, Kc 16 years old

Kc Kopaska My senior high picture
17 yrs old (Before Accident)

Walt and Ann LaDamus

Gas can from inside the jeep

Actual accident scene, the burned out
jeep and field, shortly after the fire

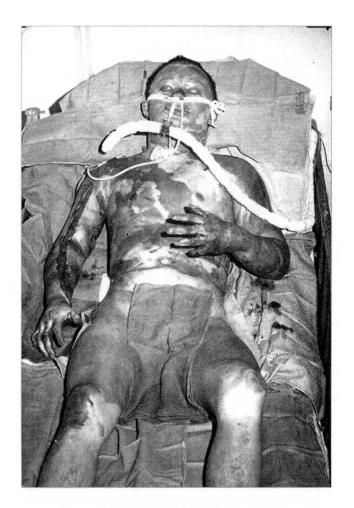

Kc, very soon after admittance to
Brooke Army Medical Center

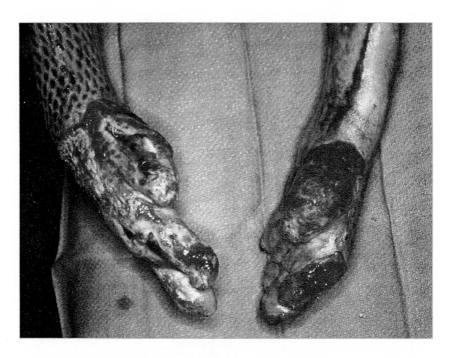

Hands after phalangeal amputations and before grafting

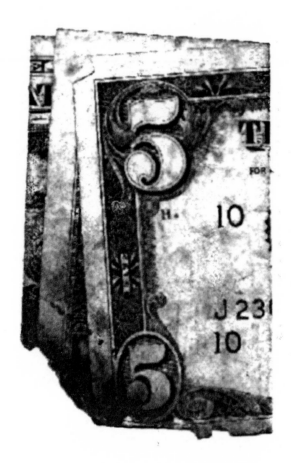

$5 bill found in my jean pocket after the accident,
only slightly burned and still intact

Kc Kopaska, high school graduation

Kc and Diane Kopaska and their children,
Cody and Kara, and son-in-law Nathan Murphy

Chapter 10

MONSTER

"**M**ommy! It's a monster!" The four-year-old cried and ran between his mother's legs. His mother grabbed his arm hard. "NO! Quiet!!" She shushed him, embarrassed, then looked me in the eye. "So sorry. He doesn't know better." But she herself could not look very long, averting her eyes from my scarred face quickly as she whisked him away.

It was my first day out in public since the accident, and we were shopping in San Antonio. Here I was, back in the outside world for the first time in three and a half months – scared, hairless, skinny as a toothpick, skin shining a cooked-lobster-bright red. I was far more ready for the public than the public was for me. Little children ran and hid when they saw me; people's mouths dropped open so wide that they could almost have stepped on their tongues.

A trial run in public was a step required by Brooke Hospital in preparation for discharge. It was mid-September. Nurses had put my arms and hands in splints and patched the holes in my skin with gauze to help ward off infections, and then wrapped an apparatus around my neck (a result of an earlier surgery). All dressed up for town in my gauze, splints, and medical apparatus, I went on my way with my brother and mother for a four-hour excursion, my first trip out into the "real world" since the accident.

Our first stop was a large department store so I could buy a hat. A second part of the assignment was to go to a restaurant. There, my mother spoon fed me like a baby. Self conscious, I noticed two men sitting a couple of tables over who could not stop staring, no matter how hard they tried. It was awkward, yes, but I didn't blame them. I looked like hell, or at the very least like I had just returned from there. Somehow, we made it through the assignment and passed with a high enough score to be allowed to go home.

I will never forget the day when I was finally able to leave Brooke for good. Three and a half months of debridement and skin grafts were over, at least temporarily. There were still years of reconstructive surgery ahead of me in Iowa, but all of that was yet to come. For today, it was exhilarating enough just to pull out of the Brooke Army Medical Center in my brother John's little Vega sedan, stuffed floor to ceiling with equipment and belongings, listening to Simon and Garfunkel's hit song, "Home."

Only we didn't go home. First, instead of going northeast to Iowa, we went northwest back to Canon City, Colorado to visit Walt, Ann, Virgil, and the scene of the accident. This place and the people in it had made an indelible impression on me, and I needed to see it all again.

Once on the road, though, the trip through Texas and New Mexico seemed to stretch endlessly on. The air was hot and dry, filled with a fine dust I never before noticed, and my body itched incessantly. I could not get comfortable and I could not sleep. Consequently, when we did stop at a motel to get some sleep, no one rested. I itched. Everywhere.

Everything from my nose to my toes itched. I think even the inside of my eyelids itched. It was a sleepless nightmare.

When we finally arrived in Canon City my Uncle Walt had a surprise for us – several quarts of homemade beer.

"Kc, I'm breaking out my best for you. I've been waiting a long time for the right occasion. Tonight is the night!"

"How old is the beer, Uncle Walt?" I asked.

"Eleven years," he replied with a big grin.

I was happy he wanted to celebrate with beer, but when he told me how old his homemade batch was, I wasn't too sure if I wanted the honor! Walt was determined, however. So with Walt's enthusiasm and the 11-year-old homemade beer, our party began.

I don't remember what we drank that night, or how much, but it was enough that I discovered a strange "benefit" of my hospitalization. The massive amounts of pharmaceuticals that had been injected into my poor body while at Brooke had increased my tolerance for alcohol; I could now handle a whole lot of booze without getting drunk!

It did not seem to be the same for some of the adults, however. Somewhere in the course of the evening, I glanced at my mother and she did not look well. I asked her how she was feeling.

"I think I need to go to bed now," she said strangely. Something told me she wasn't going to make it to the bedroom.

As Walt took her by the arm and began to lead her through the kitchen, I positioned myself behind her to catch her when she passed out. Sure enough, Mom fell straight backwards and even though I wasn't in any shape to be playing catch with her body, I nonetheless tried anyway. As she fell back, her clothing caught on one of the metal pins protruding from my right thumb. The pin ripped out, through the bone, until it was hanging by a mere thread of skin.

"What should I do?" Walt yelled.

"Don't worry about me. Is she breathing?" I responded.

"I don't know, how do I tell?" he asked.

"Put your cheek in front of her mouth. Can you feel any air coming out?" He could not.

This was about the time we both regressed from being anxious, responsible adults to panicked pre-teen boys. Thank God we didn't try to get her heart started. We would have probably hooked her up to some jumper cables.

"Give her mouth-to-mouth resuscitation!" I yelled, and for a few terrifying moments Walt proceeded to presumably breathe the life back into my unconscious mother.

After a few minutes of frantic mouth-to-mouth, Walt paused. "Something just isn't right here..." he said.

"Why not? What's she doing?" I asked.

"She's blowing air back at me!" he said, dumfounded. I burst out laughing.

"Well, then, I guess she doesn't need mouth-to-mouth!" I said.

Thank God Ann had called an ambulance while Walt and I had been heroically trying to save my mother's life. It wasn't long before it arrived and rushed us both off to the little hospital in Florence, where I had been treated the day of the accident, four months before. And who should be on call that night? Dr. Berge, the same doctor who had treated me on the day of my emergency.

He was astonished. As he finished pulling the pin out of my thumb, he looked me straight in the eye and said, "I never thought I would ever see you alive again, son. Glad to see you under better circumstances."

It turned out that my mom was mostly suffering from extreme exhaustion. The lack of sleep and pressure from caring for me had finally just played itself out. Her body didn't have one more step in it; she had to rest. We stayed at Walt and Ann's house longer than expected.

When she felt rested enough to travel, my mom and I decided to fly back to Iowa rather than attempt another long drive. Even in the airport at Sedalia, where we caught our shuttle flight to Denver, I continued to catch the attention of everyone I met, and everyone I didn't meet too. This time, my most unusual encounter began with a small Hispanic Catholic woman who approached me and began to make a scene.

"Look at this man. Look how he is all burned up." She said loudly, as she pulled her own son by the arm to face me, then reached over and grabbed my shirt, and lifted it to show her son my scars! My mother was furious. But before she could intervene, the woman continued.

"My boy, see him? He got burned too." She lifted his shirt to show me his burn scars. Indeed, her boy had some nasty scars. It was obvious the boy had tangled with some serious fire at some point in his life, also, though his injuries were not as severe as mine.

"I am going to church tonight. I will light a candle and pray for you," she said. Oddly, I was not offended by her directness, but instead, felt touched by her compassion. I felt she really cared for me, even though I was a total stranger. Her directness about my condition, and willingness to deal with it compassionately, had a surprisingly healing effect on me. In fact, it may have been one of the most significant steps toward normalizing my situation and helping me accept my new, altered self.

Finally, I arrived home and to all that Iowa meant to me. It was September now and there were small hints of fall in the air. The corn had matured and was beginning to yellow, the continuous summer symphony of crickets and other insects that harmonized during the muggy July evenings had quieted, and the leaves on the trees were just beginning to create their annual impression of brilliant red and orange sunsets.

Home was familiar, but life was not. When I walked in the door and into my kitchen, my two young nieces were there to greet me. But instead of running up and throwing their little arms around me, as they would have in the past, they stopped in their tracks when they first saw me, stunned, then cringed and backed up in fear. They didn't recognize me. I didn't look anything like the Uncle Kc they knew. This was a Monster. They wanted nothing to do with me. It was the first of many incidents that spelled out the truth – my world had radically changed and would never be the same again.

Before the summer of 1976, I revolved around life; Kc helped make life happen. Now it seemed that life revolved around me. I was unable to care for myself. I had to have my bandages changed every day. I had to be bathed in various solutions to ward off the insane itching and dry skin, and I had to be attended to day and night. No longer could I run and ride a bike. As hunting season opened, I couldn't tote a gun out in the field with one hand and grab a downed pheasant with the other.

Not long after I got home I asked my parents to throw a "Welcome Home" party for me so I could get reacquainted with my old friends. Over 200 people showed up, but about all I remember of the evening was smoking some PCP-laced marijuana and sitting by a picnic table drinking massive amounts of beer through a straw. The next thing I knew, I was waking up in bed, in the middle of the night, dying of thirst. I kicked open the refrigerator door, spotted a pitcher of beer leftover from the party, and somehow managed to get a straw in my mouth. After polishing the entire pitcher off without bothering to remove it from the refrigerator door, I made my way back to bed. This kind of drinking, waking up hung over only to begin drinking immediately again, eventually became a nasty habit that nearly killed me.

Autumn was soon upon us, and that meant hunting season. I decided to go. The delight of an early fall hunt was my first real taste of freedom since leaving Brooke. It was one of those late September days when the last of the season's grasshoppers are flitting back and forth in the weeds, blowing in the warm and lazy sun of Indian summer; when the shortened days begin to tease the reds, oranges and yellows right out of the leaves before they spread their fine carpet of color on the earth. I was really in no shape to be out hunting with Les and Craig, but I had to be out with my old friends, and out of doors. For three and a half months I had been confined inside, staring at dull, blank walls and a military white ceiling. Now, out in the late afternoon field, I breathed deeply. This is where I belonged.

I did not carry a gun that day; in fact, it was all I could do to carry myself. But none of that mattered much. I was surrounded by trees, fresh air, and an abundance of game. Many of the poor, hapless creatures we set our sights on were not listed in the hunting regulations of the Iowa's Fish and Game Department. I think we occasionally shot a fish or two. On this day, however, Les captured a great big old snapping turtle which was meandering down a dry creek bed. And believe it or not, snapping turtle is good eating!

It was hard to face the fact, though, that the things I loved and longed for were beyond my ability to do easily. It was very tiring for me to be out traipsing in the woods and pasture lands, and when we came to fences, Les would lift me up and hand me over to Craig, or vice versa. I had neither the strength nor the dexterity to maneuver a barbed-wire fence. By the time we got home, I was feeling the effects of the hunt. My skin burned from the afternoon heat, the dry air, and my shirt rubbing on it, and I was totally exhausted. Still, I had gone hunting. And I was home. Nothing else mattered – it was where I had longed to be for what seemed like an eternity.

All the little things I had taken for granted, ironically, turned out to be all the things I loved most. Someone once said, "Enjoy the little things, for one day you may look back and discover that they were the big things." Coming home was like that. It felt as if I been given a second chance to experience all the little things that are really the big things, and this time I was determined to appreciate every moment.

Chapter 11

ALONE IN A CROWD

I was finally home, but home was not the same. Something had very dramatically changed. I didn't know what it was at first, even though it was as obvious as the nose on my face, or what was left of it. Gradually, it began to dawn on me. What had changed was me.

> Humpty Dumpty sat on a wall,
> Humpty Dumpty had a great fall;
> All the King's horses and all the King's men,
> Couldn't put Humpty together again.
>
> (Classic English children's rhyme)

I was different. My life was different. Home could not give me the normalcy that I had craved since the accident. I wanted my life to be the same way that it was before I was burned and it wasn't ever going to be. How was I going to put my life back together again? I had fallen off the wall and did not even have all the king's horses and all the king's men to try and put me back together again. Simply put, I was alone. I could not envision how I would ever be able to live a normal life again. The friends and family that I had longed to be with through three and a half months of torture and homesickness were now strangers to my world of despair. It wasn't long after I got home that my old buddies began to visit me again, and reintroduce me to my old bad habits. Actually, I didn't lose those habits in Brooke; I was simply inconvenienced from satisfying them for awhile. I wasn't out of Brooke Army Medical Center for a week when I began smoking pot again and drinking as much beer as I could hold. Beer drinking became one of my favorite pastimes because, along with copious amounts of painkillers, beer helped to deaden the incessant, maddening itching that was the result of new nerve endings developing in my skin graft sites. If I drank enough, it also helped me sleep on many restless nights. Not that I needed more excuses to drink; by this time I was already an alcoholic. My friends meant to help, in their own demented way. But even when I was surrounded by them at a party, I still faced a huge, insurmountable obstacle. I was alone.

So alone. There was a lot of emotional stuff going on inside of me that I neither understood nor had any healthy coping mechanisms to manage. It would be years before I would have any training in these things, or understand that there was an emotional/mental condition known as Post Traumatic Stress Disorder (PTSD), and that I was suffering from it. Even if I had possessed any inclination to "talk about" my feelings, I would not have done so. I did not hang around with any touchy-feely people who might have surrounded me, held my hand, and sung "Kumbaya."

Besides, no one could possibly understand, or so I reasoned. While I was in the burn unit I never worried about having someone to talk to, to share my hurts or fears with. People there knew exactly what I was going through because they were suffering the same way. We had a common bond there. Our communication was as powerful during silence as it was in outbursts of anguish or despair. But outside the burn unit, that was all gone.

Loneliness is terrifying at times. There is no way to make sense out of the world around you when you are alone. There is no one with whom you can validate your thoughts and feelings, or invalidate them if need be, and get over them. In a world where you are all alone, you do not know who you are supposed to be, nor do you know how to be like anyone else. Not even your former self. I had gone from being "normal" to being "handicapped," and I did not know myself anymore. It seemed there was no one who understood. There was no one to talk to in my lonely world except for God.

And so, I talked to God, or whatever I thought "God" might be. I didn't know. I had awareness that God had His hand on my life while I was in the burn unit, but I didn't know who or what "God" was. I thought He was some indefinable, cosmic force – perhaps the power of many minds thinking about the same thing at the same time. But whatever "God" was, I talked to Him, usually late at night, or when I ran down our gravel country road.

Those times, when the physical and mental itching drove me to the brink of madness, I would run out of the house and take off down the gravel road screaming and cussing, swinging and kicking at an invisible someone, fighting the air. I would have come to the end of my rope for the moment. Even though in my own futile way I tried to tie a knot in my mind, hoping to hang onto a shred of sanity, at those moments, the knot had come untied. It felt like I was free-falling into a mental breakdown. After carrying on like this for a half mile or so, I would begin to calm down. The wild flailing of my limbs and the cursing would be replaced by a calmer disposition. I would then begin to walk and talk sensibly to my unseen "friend."

The episode would then segue into a one-sided conversation, a monologue. But it didn't feel like a monologue. It felt as though I was actually talking to someone, someone who had known me all of my life, someone who knew me better than anyone else. I would walk and talk to my "friend" for a very long time, until a deep peace would come over me. It seemed very real, as if the "friend" with me was tangible. I sensed an undeniably real presence. And at the end of these long conversations, a Voice would speak to me. It was not an audible voice, but I could hear it in my thoughts, nevertheless. It always said the same thing. "Trust and be patient. Everything is going to work out alright."

At the time, I did not recognize the presence or the voice. But looking back, after I came to a saving knowledge of Jesus Christ, I know that it was He who walked with me and talked with me when no one else could. This is incredible to me, now. I was an enemy of the cross at that time, and yet I experienced Him. Jesus walked with me, and talked with me on that gravel road. It reminds me of the verse in the Bible, Romans 5:8, "But God demonstrates His love for us in this, while we were yet sinners, Christ died for us."

There were many nights when I could not sleep. Sometimes many nights in a row. I would wander around the house and almost always end up sitting in the kitchen. It was there I would resume my conversations with God.

"Why did You do this to me? What did I do that was so bad that You had to punish me like this?" I would argue. "How am I ever going to put my life back together again?"

God never answered these type of questions; at least, I never heard Him if He did. He heard me, though; I sensed it.

While in the burn center, I experienced a hunger for God that I had never known before. His presence was very, very real, even though I wasn't a Christian and had no intentions of becoming one. But outside the center, I put all thoughts of God behind me except when I felt very frustrated, alone, or uncertain, feelings I experienced frequently.

It quickly became obvious that I needed positive structure in my life, so my parents asked the school if I could enroll for my senior year and attempt to graduate. Although I was informed that it was very unlikely that I would graduate with my classmates, the school authorities allowed me to start back to school the fall semester of my senior year. At first my old classmates looked at me with an expression of shock, but it did not take long for them to adjust and accept me back as one of their own. As they accepted me, more emotional healing began to take place.

The staff, faculty and students of Ankeny Senior High School went out of their way to help me make it through that year. It was not an easy road. In addition to all the educational complications my handicaps caused, there were many sleepless nights, and numerous periodic absences from school due to scheduled reconstructive surgeries at the larger hospital in Iowa City.

There was not a longer trip in the world than the one from Crocker to Iowa City when I was on the way to the hospital there for reconstructive surgery. No matter how I adjusted myself, I could not get comfortable in that car. If my skin was itchy, and it always was, it itched even more intensely on those trips. The music on the radio was lousy, the weather was always bad, and the car moved too slowly. The two hour trip seemed to be 20 hours long.

My surgeries were conducted by two very different doctors. The first surgeon was a cold, detached man who was always busy training interns. He left me with the impression that he was too busy training, plotting surgical strategies, and cutting on me to stop and notice that it was a human being he was working on. Often, I felt like a "cadaver" or "lab experiment" when his three or four interns examined me. It's probably a good thing, though, that I never smarted off to these guys. Who knows what anatomical adjustments they might have made while I was under the knife? But one glorious day it all changed. This surgeon informed us he would be leaving for the East Coast to start his own clinic. I felt truly sorry – sorry for the East Coast, that is. But I was more than happy to let them have him.

My next doctor was the complete opposite. Dr. Ivan Pakiam was born in India and raised, educated and married in England. By the time I met him, he was already recognized as an outstanding reconstructive surgeon. He was a gentle and soft spoken man with a distinguished English accent, whose non-threatening and supportive manner was immediately likable. Quite the opposite of my first doctor, he seemed to take a genuine interest in me as a person. He asked questions and listened to the answers. He built a level of trust with me as quickly as anyone ever has.

As much as I hated it and would have done almost anything to avoid it, I knew I could not opt out of reconstructive surgery. Repeated trips to the operating room were going to be with me for years to come. Time did not improve things; it never got any easier to go under the knife; I dreaded every single scheduled surgery. I suppose I could have thrown a fit and refused to participate, but why? I knew deep down that the emotional and physical suffering of these operations was part of the price to be paid for recovery. The surgeries not only helped to give me a functional life back, but also deposited a little steel in my soul. To this day I find myself able to face things that frighten me or seem bigger than my capabilities, tackle them, and bring them through to a satisfactory conclusion. For that, I am grateful.

After a number of reconstructive surgeries on my arms and hands, I was able to start doing some of the things again that we all take so much for granted. I was able to feed and bathe myself again, drive, go camping, and shoot a bad game of pool. I still had a very strong desire to play music, but this presented some new challenges.

I didn't think I could ever play bass guitar again, so I took up playing the steel guitar. This worked real well for awhile, until I had another surgery on my right hand. That put an end to my steel playing. My next thought was to try to play drums. I could hold the left-hand stick well enough, but had to tie the other stick to my right hand, using elastic for bounce. The right hand stick kept flipping wildly out of the elastic, threatening to do bodily harm to anyone who got in its way. In order to keep from killing somebody with an airborne stick, I quit playing drums. Well, there was always the harmonica. They'd have to cut my lips off to keep me from playing that! But harmonica playing didn't work either.

So I settled in and stuck to finishing high school. Finally, the day came. It happened. I graduated with my class, right on time, after all.

Walking across that platform to receive my high school diploma was an unforgettable moment. Emotions were running high throughout the auditorium. As my name was called, the entire audience, all in one accord, rose to its feet and filled the auditorium with the thunderous applause of a standing ovation. I was completely thrilled, fulfilled, and proud.

The people of my community were, of course, applauding much more than me that night; they were applauding a collective human victory, the victory of hope that overcomes adversity. They saw someone who had faced insurmountable obstacles and did not quit in the face of a severe trial. They saw a young man whose loss had become his gain. They saw the possibility that a person's limitations could become his strengths. But I did not do this alone; it took all of us, an entire community working together, to make this happen. When the diploma was placed in my hand, I am sure they felt as if it was placed in theirs, as well. Together, we had done this; it was "our" diploma. And together, we had all grown stronger for it.

How I wish I could have understood and cherished what was really happening that night, and embraced those values. Instead, I only valued the "party life." After achieving the goal of a high school diploma, partying became my reason for being. It also nearly became my reason for dying.

Chapter 12

RESTLESS

I t was 1981, five years after the accident, and I was restless. Deeply restless. Life had settled into a routine, but something wasn't right on the inside of me. No matter how "good" I had it, I was never satisfied. There was an aching for "more" of something inside of me, but I didn't know what "more" was. The more things I had, the less satisfied I was. It didn't matter how much I attained of the things I craved, whether drugs, alcohol, girls, cars and trucks, it was never enough. Never enough.

Then one day, as I listened to the radio, a light came on in my mind. In the popular song "Wichita Lineman," Glen Campbell sang about needing a small vacation. It clicked with me. A vacation! That was it! I needed a vacation, but not a small one, as the song said. I needed the best and longest vacation I could afford. So I set out to plan exactly that.

I planned this vacation for the summer of 1981, and I was convinced this would cure me of that restless ache. It was a six-week vacation, and it would be the best time of my life. I was going to spend four weeks in the Rocky Mountains backpacking, fishing, and climbing, followed by two weeks in California partying and running around on beaches. My insurance settlements had been extremely generous. The preceding winter I had purchased a brand new four-wheel drive pickup truck with insurance settlement money, and even after buying my dream truck, I still had plenty of money. What else was it for, but to spend?

The vacation was perfect. The mountains were majestic, the air was clean and fresh; the water that bubbled along next to many of the hiking trails was crystal clear and pure enough to slurp right out of the mountain streams. The views of wildlife were spectacular – bighorn rams butting heads on the free range in the Rockies, with huge rainbow trout scrapping with my six pound test line in the mountain streams. And California? Well, California was just as I had hoped – one big, beautiful beach party.

I truly believed that when I got back to Iowa after such an epic vacation, the restlessness would be out of my system and I would settle into contentment and peace with my life. It didn't work. Within a few days after coming home, the gnawing in my soul returned. In fact, I was even more miserable than before.

I became desperate. I ran rampant, at random, any place I willed. I hit keggers, parties, rock concerts, any place to catch a buzz. The more excitement I chased, the emptier I felt. The emptiness in my life was deepening into a void. Booze and drugs didn't fill the abyss. Friends and what few girls I got to know along the way didn't help. Hobbies like fishing, hunting, camping and mountain climbing no longer did any good. Something was wrong with me, something was eating me away from the inside out. I wanted something, or somebody, but I didn't know what or who it was, and I didn't know how to find the answer.

One August night on the way to a pig roast, this emptiness gripped me so strongly that I pulled over, stopped my truck and cried out, "God, send somebody across my path that can fill this emptiness." I know now that who I needed at that moment was Jesus Christ, but that's not who I met that night.

Instead, I met Angie.

It was a three-day party at a friend's house and there she sat with her black hair resting lazily on her shoulders. She seemed interested in me, sitting next to me, chirping away like a curious little bird exploring something it had never seen before. She was young, too young, and cute. I was stoned, hormone driven, and definitely interested in something other than her personality. I don't remember a whole lot about that particular party or what happened that night, which wasn't unusual. All I remember was that I was impressed with Angie's apparent interest in me, and the next thing I knew, I woke up on the floor of my friend's garage. I had never met Angie before; truthfully, I never expected to see her again.

As fate would have it, however, I did run into her a couple of days later when driving around Ankeny in my truck. We talked for a few minutes and I asked her out on a date; she said "yes." It was a hot August night when our date rolled around, so we took off for a beach at nearby Saylorville Lake. I often went there to swim and party with friends. With a bottle of wine in one hand and her in the other, I just knew I was in for a very pleasant evening. Boy, was I in for a surprise.

During the course of the evening we met up with Craig Argetsinger and the three of us began riding around in his Jeep. As the evening continued, both Angie and I had developed a considerable buzz from the wine. I am not sure what I said or did to trigger her, or even if I actually did anything at all, but suddenly, she began freaking out – hitting me, yelling at me – in short, she was hysterical. I was glad Craig was with us. "Help me get her home, Craig! I don't know what I did to bring this on, but this date is obviously over." Being a good friend, Craig obliged. We dropped her off at her parents' house, and Craig took me back to get my truck.

To my surprise, the next day, she contacted me. Apparently the craziness had continued at home, she had gotten into quite a tussle with her dad, and now she wanted to move out. Was I interested in sharing an apartment?

Was I interested? Even after last night's scene, living in close quarters with any member of the female species had me interested. We quickly decided to rent an apartment together, and suddenly, it seemed I had found what was missing in my life – a woman!

"So this is what was missing!" I thought. "I needed a woman of my own! It must be that I needed a woman all along to keep me happy!" What I honestly meant by "needing a woman to keep me happy" was, to be blunt, a combination of two things – the opportunity to be sexually active, and increased social status among my buddies. My view of women and sex was definitely not based on God's intended design at this time.

For a short while, my live-in girlfriend Angie and I lived a party life that knew no bounds. We actually became pretty good friends and had a lot in common – we both loved partying, liked the same TV shows and matched up on our favorite tunes. One place we didn't match, though, was in our religious roots. What I didn't know about this girl is that behind that "crazy party girl" façade was a very back-slid Christian. Everything seemed to be going along pretty well for me until one night she told me she was going back to church.

"Church!" I said. "You want to go to church? Well, whatever trips your trigger!"

Well, her trigger got tripped that night, alright. Something was different about her when she came home that night, I could tell just by looking at her. She almost glowed, and she had a joy bubbling out of her unlike anything I had ever seen in her before. Angie always laughed a lot, but now her laugh was different. It seemed to be more "real." She wasted little time in announcing to me that she had gotten "saved." I had no idea what she meant. She looked me right in the eye and told me she would be making some changes.

"Kc, I'm not going to drink with you anymore, smoke dope with you anymore, or have sex with you anymore," she said. I stood there, Budweiser in hand, trying to process what this was going to do to my lucky little arrangement. It was alright with me if she got "saved," whatever that meant. But this other stuff? I couldn't deal with it.

"There go all my fun times," I thought. For the next two weeks I tried to tear her back down to where I was. She would go to church and I would stay home and drink. She didn't get mad at me for being such a stinky old heathen, though. That impressed me.

Then one night Angie popped the question. "Will you go to church with me tonight?" The Holy Spirit is definitely stronger than a can of Budweiser, even to a seasoned drunk. I had just gotten into the refrigerator for a cold beer and had it half downed when she asked me. Even though it was totally out of character for me, I dumped the rest of the beer down the drain, turned to her and simply said, "OK."

This was completely irrational! Me? Going to church? I could have stayed home, drank cold beer, and watched "King Kong Bundy" wop the "Macho Man" upside the head. But I told her I would go, a deal had been struck; she had asked and in a weak moment I had said "OK." So now I was going to church, at least this one time.

Once inside, I was pleasantly surprised. Immediately, I felt her church was different from other churches I visited. People were smiling, happy to see each other, greeting one another with hearty handshakes and cheery dispositions. They acted like they were actually glad to be there.

When the service started they sang loudly, clapped their hands, and worshipped as if they meant business. The atmosphere reminded me more of a party than a church, which I could relate to. I began to relax, feel comfortable and let myself enjoy it. After the worship songs, the pastor invited people to come to the front and participate in "communion." I didn't really know what that was, but it looked like one more way they had fun.

"OK," I thought to myself. "I can party with these people." I went up, took a piece of bread and a little communion cup, and stepped back from the pastor who was holding one of the trays with tiny cups on it. As I stepped back, I spilled a drop of juice on the palm of my left hand. It was such a tiny amount that it didn't even change the volume level in the cup. I wouldn't have even noticed the spill at all, except for what happened next.

Suddenly, a dark purple-reddish liquid began to drip out of the palms of both of my hands. I hadn't even spilled juice on my right hand, and certainly no one else had dumped their juice on me. But the liquid just kept dripping from my palms as we walked back to our seats. A big drop splattered onto the toe of my boot. Angie was ahead of me a few steps and I wanted to grab her and ask her what was going on, but I couldn't move my hand up to do so. I looked around to get someone else's attention, but in the end I couldn't mutter even a sound, I was so stunned. About the time we worked our way back to our seats, the liquid stopped dripping. I remained speechless.

A little later the pastor preached, and believe me, I was on the edge of my seat the entire time, all ears. I didn't understand a word he said, but God had my attention. When we got home later that evening, I didn't tell Angie for fear that she would think I was nuts, so I kept it to myself. But I did tell her I wanted to learn everything I could about God. She called the youth pastor and set up an appointment for him to come over the next night and talk to me.

When I woke up the next morning, it all seemed unreal, like something I had imagined rather than something that had really occurred. Was this some kind of leftover drug hallucination? Then I remembered the boot. A big drop of that purplish-red liquid had splattered on my boot. I bolted out of my chair and ran over to the door where my boots were parked. Grabbing the boot, I flipped it up and looked straight at the toes. There it was – a large dark crimson-purplish stain, splattered right on the toe of that boot. It had happened. It was real. Adding to this odd coincidence was the strange fact that this pair of boots was the exact pair I had been wearing the day of my accident, five years earlier. My boots had somehow survived the fire, and were important to me. I cleaned them up and wore them on special occasions, like going to church for the first time. Now it seemed as though they were giving me a sign. The liquid dripping from my palms had been real; but what did it mean?

When the youth director and his wife came over that evening to talk with me, I was ready to hear what they had to say. They wasted no time. I quickly learned that I was a sinner, had always been a sinner, that I was separated from God and worthy of eternal punishment in the pit of hell. This was bad news for me. But the good news was that through

Jesus Christ I could be forgiven, united with God, and live in heaven for eternity instead. This might have been offensive to some people, but to me every single word they uttered was like a long, cool, refreshing drink of water. I just couldn't get enough of this; somehow every word they spoke was the answer to that void in my soul, and I knew it.

By the time they got around to asking me if I wanted to pray the sinner's prayer, I was like a racehorse in the gates. I couldn't wait.

We gathered in a circle, joined hands and prayed. I repented of my sinful life and asked Jesus Christ to come into my heart and take my life. As I prayed it felt as though a thousand-pound weight was being lifted from my shoulders. This was immediately followed by a joy that began bubbling up from deep inside of me. I had been high before, but this joy was unlike anything I had ever experienced in my life; it was real. In an instant, I realized I was truly "saved."

To this day, I have no doubt that I was genuinely born again that night, and that Angie also had genuinely experienced something quite similar just a few weeks earlier. We both knew we had been touched by God, and something wonderful had happened to us, but we didn't know much about what to do next with our lives and faith. Why Angie didn't move out when she first returned to her faith, I don't know. As for me, I honestly didn't realize that living with your girlfriend could be wrong, as long as you didn't have sex. We had quit having sex already because we knew that this was wrong outside of marriage. But what could be wrong with just living together as friends? It only seemed practical.

As it turned out, there was plenty wrong with it. This living arrangement was a mine field of temptation – it was inevitable that someday one or both of us would trip over a "mine" and our new faith would suffer damage. Living together kept us tied to the past. Plus, it was as though we were "keeping a foot in the door" – a door we had both decided to close. Not good. Sure enough, in time, this living arrangement became the source of our downfall. One step backward and our feet flew out from under us. It was a short slide right back down to where we had been – only further down, and in worse condition.

Chapter 13

CHOOSING LIFE

"Aw, Kc. Let's just stop and get a six-pack. A few beers won't hurt anything, as long as we don't get drunk," Angie said.

We both knew better. We were on a road trip. We had borrowed Angie's dad's car for a short trip to Missouri where we planned to decorate the grave of Angie's friend. Angie had been incarcerated in a juvenile detention center a few years earlier, and while there, her best friend had died tragically. She couldn't attend the funeral and had never visited the grave. For some reason, this was weighing heavily on her at this time, and she wanted to do it now. Our plan was to simply drive to Missouri, visit the grave, and then turn around and come right back home.

A few beers. What could it hurt? It seemed like a long time since I had a beer. It would break up the monotony of the road trip. Besides, I was an experienced drinker; I knew what I could handle and keep driving safely. I didn't put up much of a fight – in fact, no fight at all. "OK. Sounds good to me," I said.

We stopped at the next convenience store, bought a six-pack, and went on our way. Sipping our way down the highway to Missouri, we finished the six-pack somewhere close to our destination. As we had planned, we visited the grave, paid our respects, and prepared to leave. Time had gotten away from us, though. It seemed too late to turn right around and drive back home now, so we thought it best if we checked into a motel and headed back in the morning. Then it struck me. Three beers just didn't cut it. I needed more. I needed a 12-pack.

After a few more beers in the motel room, we left to find a bowling alley. In the process, I turned left in front of another vehicle and wrecked her dad's car.

I don't know what it was exactly, but something went haywire in me the night I wrecked Dave's car. It felt like just as quickly as I received Christ into my heart a few weeks earlier, I turned around and walked away from Him. It was as if I had grabbed onto Christ like He was the lip of an overhanging cliff, but I hadn't yet pulled myself all the way up on solid ground. Then suddenly, that night, I let go of the cliff, and began a moral freefall back into my old world and all of its ways. There seemed to be no brakes to slow it down, no parachute to pull this time. I sincerely wanted to be a Christian and serve Jesus Christ, but suddenly I was plummeting faster than ever before, lost, falling, and groping in the dark. It was a sick, horrible feeling, and it dogged me day after day after day.

I had not been a Christian long, but I knew that turning my back on the Christian life was the worst thing I could possibly do. I became full of guilt, conviction and anxiety. Every day was full of despair and anguish. I would get in my car and drive for hours, sobbing and crying out to God, begging Him not to let me die and go to hell. But somehow, I could not get back to the place of faith and freedom in Christ where I had been just a few weeks before.

I began drinking again. And drinking. And then I drank some more.

If Christ returned suddenly, would I be ready? I worried about this now. Recurring dreams woke me in the night, full of panic. In these dreams, Russian jets would fly overhead and just after they cleared the horizon, a bright mushroom cloud would ascend heavenward with a thundering boom. I ran to the church for safety, just as fast as I could, but I would always get there too late. Instead of being a refuge of faith, the church in my dream was full of evil, wicked people. All true Christians were gone, raptured to heaven, and I had been left behind. There was nowhere to turn.

This dream continued in its horror. I would sneak home to my house and sit in a chair, only to see the effects of radiation poisoning begin to take their toll on my body. My hair and teeth would begin to fall out. My joints would become disconnected. I would lose control of my bowels. I would sit dying in my chair, hopelessly lost, afraid of living, but even more afraid of dying.

Unfortunately, there was little relief from the fears when I awoke. These dreams were inspired by my mortal fear of going to hell, and I could not escape this fear, asleep or awake. Despite this sense of dread and horror, I still couldn't seem to turn my life back around.

Life without Jesus Christ became a gray, colorless world of depression. Every day was overcast with sadness and despair. Hope lost its power to give me a reason to live. I felt as though I was always on the inside of myself, looking out in lonely isolation. No one could enter into where I was and I had no way of escape. The world began to slow down for me and finally, I lost track of time altogether. Every day became a drunken stupor.

Because of these feelings, I drank more heavily than ever before and resorted to drug abuse like a mad man looking for an escape, some kind of peace. Trapped in guilt, I ran from God, and my mental, emotional and physical state deteriorated further. My relationship with Angie fell all to pieces as we both lost our grip on the best thing that had ever happened to us, the forgiveness of Jesus Christ. I drank so much that I quit eating altogether, and just "drank" my meals. I lost weight until I only weighed around 110 pounds. Before long, I was living on the edge of insanity and death.

One night around 10 p.m. there was a knock on the door. It was my old drinking buddy Mike.

"Hey Kc," Mike said. "Let's go have some fun." I knew Mike was inviting me on a drinking binge, but that night, for some reason, I really did not want to go.

At first I resisted, but both Angie and Mike insisted. Finally, against my better judgment, I finally gave into the pressure and got dressed to leave. Still, something about this night made me uneasy.

Mike and I drank at the local bar for several hours and then headed to his Chevy truck and sped toward South Des Moines. I had no idea where we were headed or why. All I knew was we were both pretty plastered, with two more six-packs to finish, when we were flying down a side street of Des Moines without our headlights turned on. We were too inebriated to know the difference.

Screaming through the dark, down a side street, we popped over a small hill and there, looming straight ahead at the edge of a "T" intersection, was a steep short hill. I braced myself. Mike hit the brakes. They hardly slowed the truck down at all.

Next thing I knew, I was crawling out from under the dashboard of the truck.

"Mike, you jerk!" I began swearing at Mike as he was pursing his lips, attempting to re-start the truck. It wasn't cooperating. We had laid down rubber through the intersection, jumped the guardrail and driven straight up that hill, clear to the top. It was at least 20 feet tall. Incredibly, we were both uninjured; but now we had to get the truck back down from the hill somehow.

Not knowing what else to do, we stumbled out of the wreck and began pushing it down the hill onto the street. Suddenly, there were red flashing lights.

"Quick, jump back in the truck. Switch places, you be the driver. I don't have a driver's license," Mike said.

We had no more switched places when I heard a very serious voice demanding Mike exit the passenger side of the truck. I did not turn around to see what was happening. I knew. Next, the voice was ordering me out. I reached down with my left hand, opened the door and stepped out turning to face the officer. This was definitely the wrong move.

"Move and I'll blow your head off!" the officer screamed. With his knees sharply bent in a crouched position and both arms straight out from his body, his hands were clutching a revolver pointed directly at my head. I slowly turned, put my hands on the side of the truck, and spread eagle.

We were taken off to jail that night. Drugs, booze and trouble defined all I had become. Without Jesus Christ, my life was out of control.

The straw finally broke the camel's back a few nights later when I commenced to choking Angie.

That evening I drank myself into a state of unconsciousness, after which Angie left for a night on the town. About 10 or 11 p.m. some friends dropped by with a bottle of tequila.

Already drunk, I drank straight shots of tequila, draining it clear down to the worm at the bottom of the bottle. By the time Angie finally returned, I was angry with her, for some reason. In my opinion, she had been out too late, and I took her in the bedroom and began choking her and throwing her around the room. She finally escaped and called my parents to come over and calm me down.

In the morning, my mom showed up at the door. "Do you think you have a problem, Kc?" she asked.

"Yeah, I know I have a problem," I said.

"Are you ready to get help?"

"Yeah," I said. I was ready to cooperate.

"Then let's go, Kc," she said, and we packed up my things and left the apartment. She was taking me to a psychiatric center for an evaluation. Even though the sun was shining bright on that calm winter afternoon, it was one of the grayest days of my life. As I sat staring out the window of the car, tears trickling down my cheeks, I could find nothing within myself or see anything outside of myself that gave me a reason to want to be alive. The dark gloom of depression had swallowed up my joy. I felt lifeless, drained. All of the color had gone from my life.

After being admitted to the psychiatric center, I was diagnosed with clinical depression and suicidal tendencies. I don't recall wanting to kill myself, but I do recall not particularly wanting to live. Without Jesus, what was there to live for? Booze, drugs, sex, money, a great vehicle – I had it all, and all of it had let me down. What else did the world have to offer?

They admitted me to the center and put me under the care of a staff psychiatrist. He wasn't much help. He kept trying to "make me happy" with external things, but I knew that "happiness" wasn't enough. I would never find happiness without Jesus. All I wanted in that psych center was my Bible. My mom brought me the Bible I had been given as a child by the Methodist Church.

At night, after everyone was quietly in bed, I would sit up, read my Bible and talk to God. One night I was going through this routine when suddenly, I had a flashback. I stood up next to my bed and was somehow transported back to that moment in the Colorado field, right after the wreck, when my body was a flaming torch, and I had a life-or-death decision to make. Once again, this time in the psych ward instead of a field, Time seemed to stop. I had the same moment of mental clarity as I had that day in the fire, when my mind lay before me a life-or-death choice. The first time the choice had been "I can inhale this fire and die, or I can fight through this but never be the same again." In this moment, my parallel choice was "I can deny Jesus and die by ending it all myself, or I can accept Jesus back into my heart, start a new life and truly live for Him."

Again, it was a pivotal moment, and I sensed that same Someone asking me, "So what will you choose? Will it be life or will it be death?"

Life. All I wanted was Life.

This time, I chose Jesus.

Quickly, I dropped to my knees and prayed "Jesus, I just want you." Five little words, the simplest prayer of my life. Then I fell asleep. When I woke up I was a different person.

Within days, I was released from the psych center, just two weeks after being admitted.

My first visit when I arrived in Ankeny was to the pastor of the church I had previously attended. I asked him if he would pray for me, and standing there in the parking lot of the church, right by my car, he did. He led me through a prayer in which I formally rededicated my life to Christ. Not that I needed to, the issue was settled for me. I suppose he thought it was necessary insurance.

My second visit was to Angie. I went straight to my apartment and found her there, sitting in an easy chair, next to the wall. "Angie, I want to get my life right and live for Jesus. What do you want to do?" I asked.

She looked up at me, straight into my eyes, and said, "I want to live for myself."

A shockwave of disappointment and unbelief washed over me. I had not expected this from the girl who led me to church. She said it with such a strangely casual tone. I knew she meant it, and I also knew that it meant we were through.

"Ok, Angie, that's up to you. But you'll have to serve yourself someplace else," I said.

It wasn't easy letting go of Angie, but I had to let go of her to maintain my walk with Christ. She packed up and was on her way to her parents' house by the end of the day. Without her companionship, as messed up as it was at times, I found myself in an isolated, lonely predicament. I didn't really have any Christian friends, none of my family members were serving Christ, and I didn't dare go back to my party buddies. Except for Christ, I was alone. For the time being, I was OK with that. I meant it when I prayed at the hospital, "Jesus, I just want you."

It's a good thing, too. Because for a short while, after finally trudging out of the pits of self-destruction and depression that had defined most of my life, Jesus was all I had.

Chapter 14

BEGINNING AGAIN

The day after giving Angie the boot, I pulled into the parking lot of my apartment and there, leaning against his Jeep, was my old friend Craig Argetsinger.

"Hey, Kc, let's go four-wheeling and drinking,." he yelled at me as I got out of my car.

"I can't do that anymore," I replied. "I'm a Christian now."

"A what?!" he exclaimed. And with that, began to pummel me with a barrage of cuss words as well as make references to me being a sandal-wearing "Jesus Freak." When he realized I actually did have on an old pair of flip-flops, he came unglued at the seams. I was not prepared for this. My best childhood friend was practically in my face, hurling a very earnest, verbal assault at me, and I had no idea how to handle it.

I took a deep breath and stepped back. Then, in a flash, I understood. Craig was not really angry at me, he was angry at himself. He had been raised a good Catholic boy and he knew the way we had been living was not right. His Catholic faith had not yet let go of him, though he had let go of it many years before. At my announcement, he was the one who didn't know how to respond. So he went with the reaction he knew best – anger and cussing. He did not know how else to handle this change in me. Besides that, he had a very short fuse. I once watched him beat a boy bloody for accusing him of putting dirt and gravel in his gas tank, thus resulting in a blown engine. Funny thing was, it was true. I know. I helped him do it. But Craig thrashed that boy right in front of his own parents, anyway, just because the kid made him mad. I had every reason to be somewhat afraid of Craig when he was angry like this.

Even so, at the moment Craig was yelling at me, I felt no sense of danger, anger, or even rejection. Instead, God gave me a sympathetic glance into my old friend's soul. All I could feel was pity and sadness. I did not see Craig very often after that encounter. In fact, not again until spring break of my first year in Bible college.

From this point as a blazing new Christian, I became crazy in a whole new way, complete with Jesus t-shirts and evangelism tracts. These were the days when the "Moonies" were out in droves, evangelizing the world. Moonies were members of a cult that was started by a Korean named Sun Myung Moon in 1954. He believed that he was the second coming of Christ, and taught that anyone that was not a follower of him was an agent of Satan. Moonies were mostly known for dressing in sandals and long white robes, standing on street corners and in airports where they would hand out little fake flowers and their own version of evangelistic literature. I thought if they could do this, then so could I, minus sandals and long white robes.

At least once a week I would drive south to the Des Moines airport, find a Moony, park myself right beside him, and then do my best to beat him to as many people as I could that were departing their flights. They were taught to be peaceful, non-confrontational people, which gave me a great advantage. I wasn't. No matter how mad tired passengers got at me, I would stay after them until they took my tract. Finally, the airport had enough of all of us and kicked us out of there. It did not bother me to get kicked out of the airport; I just headed downtown and took aim on overworked business people.

Suddenly, I was obsessed with the Bible. The book came alive to me; its stories and truths jumped off the pages every time I read it, as it if had been just written. One night, I was sitting at my kitchen table reading about the crucifixion of Jesus Christ, when it became personal.

"He's doing that for me," I realized. There they were, spitting on Him, slapping Him, beating Him…and somehow, it became real to me for the first time. He went through all of this for me, Kc Kopaska. As I read about His flogging, when they were beating Him mercilessly, I was transported emotionally and mentally to my experiences in the Hubbard Tank – twice a day, when they peeled off my burned flesh, and I was literally skinned alive. Deep inside, I intuitively understood what Jesus felt on the cross. I felt this so deeply that it caused me to question God.

"Why, God?" I questioned out loud. "Why would You do that to Your own son, God? Why would You allow them to do this?"

Then I read on, and the soldiers stretched Jesus out of the cross and nailed Him there to die. All at once, I felt the nails, too. As I was reeling from the anguish of the cross, God spoke to me very quietly; inwardly. I heard the thought: "I did this because I love you."

From that moment on, it was settled in my heart – I would love this God forever. After that night, I became an obnoxious pain to everyone in my church by obsessively, constantly asking them how I could serve God more, and do it better.

Not only did I beg for more training, but I constantly harassed other fellow parishioners for not doing enough. The most common response of my fellow church members was something along the lines of, "Kc! We should lock you up for the next six months! But don't worry! Soon you'll get past this radical "new believer" stage and calm down like the rest of us."

Of course, that did not appeal to me at all. The more they told me to calm down, the more I stepped it up. I was deeply grateful for a second chance at life, and there was a fire burning inside of me. I most certainly did not want to "calm down" like everyone else! I was determined that, one way or another, I would save the world. Little did I know that the fire burning inside of me was more than "a stage"; it was also an indicator that I had a "calling" on my life to full-time ministry.

In all fairness, those poor everyday church folks were not prepared for the persistent pounding over the head I was giving them. Finally, after only a couple of months of attending the church at every possible opportunity, a wise couple in the church, Jerry and Kay Marlow, came to everyone's rescue. Jerry, with a slight hint of irritation, told me that if I wanted to do something great for God, I needed to go away to Bible college.

Bible college? I hated college, any kind of college. I had earlier attended a two-year community college for several semesters after high school, but it was just another place to find parties, drugs, and girls. As far as I was concerned, a college education wasn't worth the effort. When I finally decided to totally relinquish my will to God's plan for my life, it was without any desire or plan to further my education.

"Bible college?" I asked. I had never heard of such a thing. Thinking perhaps there were none close enough to be practical, I pretended to be open minded. "Well, where is the closest one?"

"There's a good Bible college right up in Des Moines," Kay said. That was not what I wanted to hear. This Bible college was accessible and close to home; in fact, way too close to home. Now I had no excuse not to go.

If you fly low over Polk County, Iowa, I am sure you can still see the heel marks that I left as God dragged me from Ankeny to Des Moines to enroll in classes at Open Bible College. (This school is now defunct, and no, I did not "defunct" it!) I waited right up to the deadline before depositing myself in my Chevrolet Chevette (Believe me, I would have much rather said Corvette, but at least my little "girly" car had a four on the floor!) and driving there in time to enroll for the 1981 fall semester. Other than assuming that this was the pathway to the ministry, I did not have a clue as to what field I should study at a "Bible college." On top of that, I dreaded the idea of once again becoming a student. Still, I really did know deep down in my heart that I was supposed to do this.

When I stepped up to enroll, my academic advisor asked, "What program do you want to enter?"

"I don't know," was my casual response.

"Well, we'll just sign you up under Pastoral Studies," he replied.

That settled it. "Pastoral Studies" – well, it had a ring to it, and at least I now had a college major. I stuck with Pastoral Studies until I graduated.

It was my first day of Bible college; and if I would have thought too much about it on that day, it would have been my last. I never did like school, ever. In my view, school was evil. The only reason I liked going at all after sixth grade was because it was an easy place to buy drugs.

Of course, my motivation for being in school was quite different now. During my first class as a new student I attempted to look on the bright side as I sat at my desk looking down at a Bible. Suddenly, it occurred to me that Bible college would be a piece of cake.

"Hey, how hard can this be? It's only one book," I comforted myself. Little did I know all the ways contrived to "educate" us in the intricacies of that book.

My short-term memory was impaired from years of drug and alcohol abuse, I had no discipline to study, and on top of that, I had to compete in classes with a bunch of "church brats," many of whom also attended private Christian schools and came to Bible college knowing all the "right" answers. I became the "non-conformist" student who looked at things in a different way. Since I didn't know "the right answers," I wanted to know how to find answers for myself. For a kid like me, I have to admit that Bible college seemed oddly like hell at times! No wonder I was opposed to it. There was no turning back, however; I felt that out of obedience to the Lord I had to finish a four-year degree there. I was determined not to let Him down.

The first three years were very difficult. Back then, instructors used a grading system called the "bell curve" that, among other things, limited their ability to reward a student for extra effort. Without going into too much detail, the bell curve essentially assigned a student's grade based on the performance of other students, instead of their raw percentages on work turned in. The bell curve assumption was that most students would perform at the common percentage, C's, which represented the apex of the curve or the top of the bell-shaped graph. A lower percentage of students were assigned grades at either end, in the low or high grade range. The system artificially predetermined that only a small percentage of students could receive either failing or excellent grades, F's and A's respectively. To put it simply, even if my test and assignment performance improved throughout the duration of the class, if just a few students scored high grades that extra effort rarely paid off. Pitted against the "church brats," it seemed to me that I didn't stand a chance. This caused me a great deal of frustration because no matter how hard I studied, I almost always ended up in the "C" percentile. I felt I deserved better. The "bell curve" grading system was strangely de-motivating.

Another thing that caused me a good deal of consternation was that I knew that there were a few instructors who more or less pulled their lectures from old seminary notes without doing their own homework. In other words, they could not explain how they arrived at a particular theological conclusion. I have an extremely inquisitive mind. I was not nearly as concerned about a particular conclusion or statement a professor expressed, as much as I was about how the professor arrived at that belief. If I thought one of them was simply reciting stuff from memory, I would hammer them with a barrage of questions that I was pretty sure ahead of time they could not answer. I was yelled at in class a few times for doing this, but I really didn't care. I often thought to myself, "If I ever teach I will not grade students on a curve against each other; I will also evaluate student performance more on effort than on performance, and I am also going to know the 'whys' behind any information before I divulge it!" Of course, it was ridiculous of me to even think in these terms. There was no way I could ever become a teacher.

Finally, there came a bright side in my first year of Bible college – spring break.

Since my first year of Bible college was such an adjustment, spring break couldn't come fast enough for me. During my time away from classes, I planned to spend the week camping at Jester Park, one of my favorite old stomping grounds. I was looking forward to no books, no assignments, and best of all, no people! Then God changed my plans for me. My spring break was to include one other person.

As I drove toward my destination, across the mile-long bridge that spanned Saylorville Lake, I spotted a familiar face. It was my old friend Craig Argetsinger, driving toward me in his Jeep. I stopped my car right there on the bridge, as did Craig, and asked him if he wanted to go camping with me. To my surprise, he said "Yes."

While Craig and I were camped out at Jester Park, we spent the better part of three days mostly talking about God and His Word. I even have a photograph of him sitting at a picnic table reading my Bible. We had a glorious time together. We were like those two innocent kids in the tent again, gazing at the stars at night. This time we mused a little more maturely, about the meaning of life, the love of God, and salvation in Jesus Christ, instead of about shooting stars and imaginary civilizations so very far away. Yes, Craig was back, my once-in-a-lifetime friend. Craig was still Craig, Kc was still Kc, and our friendship was restored.

One night, while we were out walking the trails (there weren't any railroad tracks available), a marauding raccoon got into my stuff and pulled out a loaf of bread, part of which it ate. We found the partially consumed loaf a short distance down a nearby trail. Suddenly I heard a strange grinding sound. It was Craig engaging his brain.

"Hey, let's get some of the treble hooks out of your tackle box, tie them together, and string them through the loaf of bread. Then, we can tie it to this branch just over the picnic table and catch him," he said with strange sort of grin.

"Oh sure," I thought out loud. "And who's gonna unhook it?" I asked, knowing without a doubt that he had me in mind. Raccoons do not need much of a reason to tear a person to shreds. I was not about to take hold of one with sharp fishing hooks protruding out of its body. After a good laugh, Craig's "great idea" was quickly trashed.

I did not pray with Craig about his relationship with Christ during that camping trip, but he acted with a new respect toward me afterward, and God graciously redeemed our friendship. I really do not know what fruit was produced out of that time spent with my old neighbor during that spring break. I wish I did. Craig suddenly dropped dead of a heart attack at work the spring of 1997.

Chapter 15

PRICELESS

"Ready for lunch, Diane? It's still a little early," Tammy asked her roommate.

"Yeah," Diane said. "Let's go on over. The cafeteria gets crowded fast at lunch now with all the new students. Maybe we'll get a better table and have a chance to meet some of them if we get there early."

It was the start of a new year at Open Bible College, the perfect time to scout out everything new on campus, especially the "new guys." Tammy and Diane were busy upperclassman, but what could be more interesting during the first week of school than the new personalities and possibilities that a fresh class of students brings?

The girls got their food, picked a table, and were looking around for friends when a certain young man caught Diane's eye, and for a moment she could do nothing but stare. This was not a typical stare of interest, however. Instead, it was an unavoidable stare. What she saw made her stomach nervous.

There, with a table full of guys, sat a young man whose entire face had been eaten away by fire. At first glance, his face looked like a mass of scars; he had no ears, and his hands were nubs from the second finger joint down.

"What?" Tammy asked, as she noticed Diane had stopped talking. She followed Diane's eyes to the neighboring table.

By this time, the other girls joining them at the table also joined the stare. The young man was turned away from them just enough that he either didn't see the girls staring at him, or he just didn't care.

In a split second Diane looked away and quickly glanced back at the girls at her table. "Did you see him?" she whispered. "I wonder what happened?"

"Yeah...let's talk about it later," Tammy said. "It won't be so awkward." The girls finished up quickly and left the cafeteria.

They soon found out that the young man's name was Kc. He had been sitting there, in the cafeteria, eating like he didn't have a care in the world. He sat with a table full of guys having a conversation with them, oblivious to the "storm" his appearance caused.

That night, as Tammy and Diane were getting ready for bed, they talked about the young man they had seen earlier in the day.

"Do you think you could ever marry someone like Kc?" Diane asked.

After a few thoughtful seconds Tammy replied, "I could if that was God's will for my life."

Diane was troubled. "To be honest, I don't know if I could. I don't know if I could marry anyone with an obvious disability," she said. "And that bothers me."

For several days Diane could not rest. She knew it should not be the outward appearance that counted, but what was on the inside of a man. She knew this in her head, but knowing it in her heart was clearly another matter.

The idea wouldn't leave her alone. She began to pray, and pray hard, about the idea of "marrying someone like that." After a long and restless week, she finally made peace with the concept. She believed that God had a plan for her life, and realized that she could be happy with whatever God wanted, even if that meant marrying someone with an obvious disability. Little did she realize what a critical preparation this was for her future. Two years later, Diane found herself at this crossroads again, when Kc Kopaska proposed and asked her to share the adventure of being his wife.

****

So, what's a guy to do? During my junior year of Bible college, I and another male student at Open Bible College made an astute observation. There were a lot of single girls at this college, and no one was dating them. We each made a list, checked it twice, and decided that we would date every one of them until we got through our lists. Seemed like a worthy goal to me.

I started working through mine on a warm, autumn Friday night with a girl named Onalissa. She was a bit younger than me, which was good, and was respectably cute but had the culinary taste of a stray dog. I took her to a nice restaurant called Stephen's that was built to look like a castle, complete with a moat and fake drawbridge. I ordered the filet mignon and she ordered a hamburger.

That next day, Saturday, I was flat broke but undeterred to reach my goal. I asked out another girl named Diane with whom I had been hanging out on campus for several weeks.

I treated her to a high-end seafood place. She ordered the lobster. Now I had a bona fide conundrum on my hands. If I continued dating either one, I had a choice to make – should I choose the one that was cheaper to feed but with poor taste, or the one who didn't realize that I was poorer than a church mouse but had good taste? I chose the latter. I had easily tricked Diane into thinking that I had money, and we enjoyed the same kinds of food. What could be more important to a budding relationship? We were off to a good start. Now, I just had to figure out how to cover the check I floated to pay for the unfortunate crustaceans.

Diane was as far as I got on that list. We dated a few more times after that particular Saturday; well, to be honest, we saw each other every night for the next few weeks! You could say we were "ready" for each other, but this was a strange paradox. We were "ready" for each other because neither of us "needed" each other. In our separate journeys, we had individually decided that the most important relationship in our life was our personal relationship with God. We both wanted to marry someday, but had decided that developing an intimate relationship with God was more important than marriage. For me, this peace was hard won, and followed months of wondering if any woman would truly want to wake every morning to a face like mine. It seems funny now that I could, on the one hand, exude the confidence and audacity to think I could date an entire campus full of single women, albeit a small campus, and on the other hand inwardly doubt that I could actually win one of their hands in marriage. I deeply wanted someone with whom to share my life. But after much time spent in prayer and self-reflection, I finally came to grips with the idea that I could be content never to marry as long as I was able to serve God with my life. He genuinely was enough. Diane, during the same period of time, had reached the same conclusion for herself.

So now I had a problem. Within two weeks of our first date, I sensed that we were meant to spend the rest of our lives together. You might think I would have been pleasantly surprised at this turn of events, but I was actually a little mad at God over the whole thing. I had really wrestled with the idea of never being married. It took a lot of hard work in order to make peace with the idea of remaining single, and now, all of the sudden, it seemed all of that emotional distress was for nothing! One night as I walked down the hall toward my bedroom, I said, "Lord, if you want me to marry this woman, You're gonna have to change me." I really don't know what I meant by that brief prayer, and I don't know what He did to me as I slept that night, but when I awoke the next morning, I felt changed. I can't tell you what changed or how I changed. I just felt changed. One thing was for certain – I knew beyond a shadow of a doubt that I was supposed to marry Diane. And, I must say, I felt really good about that. Ours was genuinely a union made in heaven.

Diane is priceless, a gift from God. Often, I have imagined Him digging through a huge treasure chest, intently looking for just the right woman for me. After He had dug down deep enough and found the perfect jewel, He pulled it out and gave it to me for my sole possession to cherish and care for as long as I had breath to do so. On July 16th of 1983, Diane's uncle, Fritz Zimbelman, performed the ceremony that would unite us once and for all. After more than 25 years of marriage to her, my feelings have only intensified. I love to tease Diane by telling others, "Boy, was she lucky," but there is never any doubt in anyone's mind who the lucky one was.

When we married the summer between my sophomore and junior years, Diane had graduated and I had two years of undergraduate college left. This meant, of course, that she had to help put me through the remaining two years of my bachelor's degree. By the end of my junior year, she told me in no uncertain terms that she was tired of the Bible college scene and could not wait until it was over. A funny thing happened, however, toward the end of my junior year. I felt a very strong prompting from the Lord to further my education and get a master's degree.

"If you want me to go to seminary, you are going to have to tell Diane. I'm not going to." I told God very clearly, in one of those less pious prayer moments that frequently earmark my conversations with God. I did not say a word about it to Diane for a very long time after that.

One evening, while we were lying in bed talking about life in general, I felt it was time to broach the subject of going on to seminary. Not knowing how she would respond, I said to her in a calm voice, "I think I am supposed to get more education."

Without hesitation, she responded in a similar tone, "I know." To this day I have never asked her how she knew. I was grateful that she was sensitive enough to the prompting of the Holy Spirit that I did not have to persuade her.

Soon after graduating from Open Bible College, we loaded up the truck and headed to a well respected theological seminary. Though I had knuckled down my senior year of Bible college and managed to pull my grades up to A's and B's, my overall grade point average was so low that I entered seminary on academic probation. After a few weeks in seminary, however, I discovered that I was actually fairly intelligent. This, despite one of my college professor's best efforts to discourage me from enrolling in seminary – period. He told me that I should not attend seminary because it was reserved for the "cream of the crop," implying that I was not one of those floating at the top of the milk can.

So, I was in seminary. I applied myself, studied hard, and was very shortly bored to death. In one respect, seminary was even worse than Bible college. I was itching to be out in the real world conquering mountains for the Kingdom of God, but here I was back in a stack of books again. To make matters even more miserable, I had no more insight as to why I was at seminary than I did about why I had been in Bible college. I was simply there out of obedience. Toward the completion of my master's degree in Biblical Literature, I thought that I was seeing the end of this agonizing monotony. Finally, I could get on with whatever it was God wanted me to do.

There are some days when I think cussing and kicking the neighbor's dog (provided you don't have one of your own) ought to be standard fare for trying to follow God's will. I didn't own a dog, just a mentally challenged cat named Spot. But there was a day like that toward the end of my time in seminary. Once again, I felt that gentle nudge to take my academic life one step further – this time, I sensed I was to pursue a Master of Divinity, a degree requiring twice as many credit hours as my MA, though, some of those credits were transferable. I enrolled in the Missiology track with a second concentration in Biblical Languages, i.e., Greek, Hebrew, and Aramaic. But why was God leading me to get all of this education? It seemed at the time that perhaps the most valuable education I was getting was a graduate degree in the fields of "trust, obedience, and faith." I decided that those were the three most important prerequisites to fulltime ministry, anyway.

I did what I had to do to get through – studied, wrote lots of papers, and worked outside jobs. Then along came Cody. Diane decided that we had waited long enough. It was time to add to the family. When we were first married and planning our future together, we both thought it wise to wait about five years before conceiving our first child. We wanted to delay this wonderful event in order to give ourselves adequate time to get to know each other and to give me time to finish my education, which, at the time, we thought would take only another couple of years.

On April 12th of 1988, God gave us a redheaded little boy whom we named Cody. And I do mean "little." He got a bit too anxious to introduce himself to the world, jumping the gun by about six weeks. While we were walking through a K-mart store in the middle of her eighth month of pregnancy, Diane's water suddenly broke. It was a real gully washer. Evidently, he had kicked a hole in the fetal membrane. We did our best to discretely exit the store and headed straight for the hospital.

Once we arrived at the hospital, Cody decided he would take his time with the rest of the performance, causing Diane to experience a long, drawn-out delivery. As the final moments approached, however, I was standing by her bed listening to his heart monitor when, just before he was delivered, the monitor went silent. The doctor and his attending nurses looked anxious. He grabbed a pair of forceps and quickly yanked Cody the rest of the way out. Evidently, Diane's amniotic fluid had drained so quickly that it had washed the umbilical cord down around his neck, causing him to be strangled as he was coming through the birth canal. He came into the world weighing four pounds eight ounces and squealing like a wounded rabbit. Thankfully, other than a little jaundice, he suffered no long-term effects.

After her maternity leave was over, she went back to work. I always got home after classes before she got out of work. I would immediately head across the street to the babysitter's to pick up Cody, attend to his needs, and try to get in as much study time as possible before heading to work in the evening. Often times I would arrive home in the morning, after working all night, just in time to shower and head to classes, and then head back home in order to start the process all over again. Sleep was at a premium. Many days I was lucky to squeeze in three or four hours of sleep. This routine was exhausting, to say the least, but there was light at the end of the tunnel. My degree program was nearing its end. That being the case, there was still one little problem I had not yet solved. Why in the world did I need all of this education? One day the answer came to me from an obvious but overlooked source, Diane's dad.

Not long before finishing my M.Div., he told me about a small Native American Bible college that he had financially supported for years. Diane and I had been married for about five years by this time and I do not recall him ever mentioning the place before. When he mentioned it that day, though, it was as though the lights came on. Suddenly, all the education made sense. I was called to Native Americans and was to begin my life-long ministry as an instructor at Central Indian Bible College (CIBC) in the remote town of Mobridge, South Dakota, located just 40 miles south of the North Dakota border. Teaching in a Bible college required both the MA and M.Div. degrees.

Native American Ministry. Why would a burned up Iowa kid like me be suited for working on a reservation? Would the strong and proud Native Americans even listen to a white man with nothing but scars for a face? Why would they listen to a white man who had no hands or ears? It was a mystery to me, but the doors began to open. Soon, I was hired at CIBC, and we were on our way to a culture as foreign to us as we were to them. We might as well have been leaving the country as missionaries heading to another continent. I knew nothing about the Native American people, but I was about to discover that my scars held a secret to gaining their trust, opening doors of friendship with these brave but deeply wounded people.

Chapter 16

BRANDED BY AN EMBER

"If you will come with me on visitation, I will teach you about my people." I looked up from my teacher's desk into the face of a Native American son. This was a man whose face told a story. He was one of the older students at CIBC, and his name was Eugene King. Eugene was a full-blooded Nakota Sioux from the Sisseton-Wahpeton Reservation, located in the Northeast corner of the state. I was Eugene's instructor, but Eugene was about to become my mentor.

I have no doubt God sent him to me. Pastor King, as he is most often referred to by his people, was the pastor of a small congregation in the village of Wakpala on the Standing Rock Reservation. I knew virtually nothing about Native American culture and was certainly not about to turn down his offer. "When do we leave?" I asked.

"I'll meet you here on Saturday," he said.

That Saturday, I rode with him out to the church. It was an old bank building that, had it not been designated a historical landmark, would most certainly have been torn down years ago. It was a wreck of a place, without even an indoor bathroom, just an old outhouse out back of the church. But this is where Eugene's people worshiped.

I quickly learned that the first order of business was to spend a half an hour or so in prayer before heading out. I knelt down on one of the old pews, bowed my head, and before I uttered a sound I heard an inner voice speak to me.

It said, "If you go out on visitation today, you will die."

I paused for a moment. Was this a divine warning? Something about this thought seemed odd to me. Suddenly, I knew how to handle it. My silent prayer became, "God, if this is You giving me some kind of a warning, then I am not afraid to die, and ready to come home. But devil, if this is you, you are going to have to do better than that to keep me from ministering to these people."

I bowed my head again, prayed aloud that we would touch lives in a meaningful way for the Lord, and then left, in tow of Eugene. Wouldn't you know it? Not a single life-threatening thing happened. Thus began my cross-cultural training among the Lakota people of the Standing Rock Reservation, and the most meaningful friendship I have ever experienced. It continues to this day. God willing, within the next year or two, I will be helping my old friend Eugene build a new church in Wakpala.

Though I did not doubt that I had a calling to Native American ministries, I still thought about other possibilities in the ministry. I am not one for doing the same thing for long periods of time. I am good at starting projects and programs, but once they are up and running I get bored and move on to the next world-shaking idea that pops into my mind. In other words, I'm the kind of guy that has a dozen or so half-finished projects lying around the place that lost my interest somewhere between loosening the first screw and slapping on the last coat of paint. In conversations, if a person doesn't get to the point quickly, they might as well be talking to a doorknob. My mind is somewhere else. Sermons? Forget it. I think there ought to be a law against preaching that lasts longer than ten minutes at a time, and that's stretching it.

A few weeks into our weekly Saturday visitations to Wakpala, which primarily consisted of knocking on people's doors and asking them if we could come in and pray with them (and occasionally providing food items if they were in really desperate straits), we drove down a rutted, dirt road to a broken-down house on the outskirts of the village. Close to our destination, we passed by the charred foundation of a house that, judging by the weeds and saplings that had grown in and around it, had burned down some time ago. Inside of the home we were visiting lived a frail, elderly Indian woman and countless cats that had long ago out-used their kitty litter box. As I sat down on the couch in her living room, I noticed a blanket that had been secured over the doorway between the kitchen and living room, swaying slightly in the winter wind making its way through gaps around the windows and outside doors. Next to me, sitting on a stand, was a bottle of lice shampoo. I had followed Eugene into the world of extreme reservation poverty.

After visiting the elderly woman a couple more times and feeling comfortable enough to carry on a conversation with her, I asked her about the story behind the charred foundation, visible not far from her front door. With her head bowed down and her eyes fixed on the floor, she told me the story.

One very cold wintry day her daughter, who had lived there, got very drunk. In her stupor, she threw a few pieces of wood into the wood-burning stove that heated the place but neglected to close the stove's door. Soon after putting the wood in the stove, she picked up her little infant and proceeded to pass out on the couch in the same room as the stove, baby clutched tightly in her arms. The stove was unforgiving of her carelessness.

An ember from the crackling fire popped out of the stove and landed in some tinder and papers on the floor nearby. The woman told me that she happened to look outside toward her daughter's house and spotted dark smoke pouring out of it. She quickly ran to the house, made her way inside, and tried to awaken her. Failing to do so, she grabbed hold of her and tried to pull her outside but was too weak to do that, too. In a final act of desperation, she gave up on her daughter and tried with all of her might to free the baby from her daughter's arms in an attempt to save at least one life. I could tell by the subtle shift in her tone of voice that she felt shame and responsibility for not having enough strength to even save her granddaughter. She raised her head a little bit and glanced my way when she finished her story by telling me, "The only thing I could do was back out of the burning house and watch as it took my daughter and grandbaby."

There was a pause. I did not say anything in response. I didn't need to. She knew I understood something about fire. It was my scars that had opened the door. The fact that she even told me the story meant that she knew she could trust me with it. I felt that by sharing it with me that a little bit of the sharp edges of her pain and grief had been dulled, even if just for a moment. That was the day I realized, as I drove away from her home, past the charred foundation, that I would always belong to these people. My calling to Native American ministries was secured, once and for all, branded on my heart by an ember. I had suffered much in life and now I saw a reason for my scars – they could proclaim Christ in a way that words never would. God would use my pain to bring healing to their nations. Ever since that day, I have carried with me a deep sense of privilege to bear these scars for His cause.

From Eugene I learned many inside cultural cues about his people; about eye contact, use of humor, the importance of meals, and most of all, how to love people with a depth of service and faithfulness that set the bar very high for me in my own ministry. With the start of our cultural indoctrination, Diane and I said "yes" to a request to pastor the church on the Lower Brule Reservation, 160 miles south of Mobridge. We were happy to go, but were not well received. It turned out the Anglo pastor before us had earned three consecutive 30- year sentences for molesting Native American children. Naturally, the folks in the native community automatically associated us with him. Our very first day in Lower Brule, while just sitting down for dinner, an Indian gentleman burst through the front door and began ranting and raving at us in his language. We had an interpreter there named Blind Ernie, who finally escorted him outside where we could still hear him yelling. Finally, Ernie came back inside.

"What was he saying?" I asked Ernie.

He responded, "He said he was going to go home, get his shotgun, and come back and kill all of us."

"Well, at least that should give me time to finish my dinner before I die," I thought to myself. And with that I forgot about the whole affair. He never returned.

Eugene's practical and compassionate ministry methodology quickly wore off on us. Diane and I decided we were going to simply pray for our few parishioners and anyone else who would let us, serve them all with the few resources that we had, and teach them what we could about Jesus. Eugene never confronted his people about their native religious and traditional ways, and neither did we, especially as Anglos. As simple as our approach was, the ministry to the people of Lower Brule was still exhausting. We would work at the school all week, then jump in the car on Friday afternoon and drive 160 miles south. On Friday night I conducted a Bible study, followed by visitation all day Saturday, and two services on Sunday. Then we drove home Sunday night in order to get up Monday morning, start the school week, and begin the process all over again.

Diane and I started ministering in South Dakota under a temporary missions program in 1989. After a year and a half there, we were promoted to a more permanent position with our denomination, and given permission to begin traveling to various churches around the country in order to raise monthly financial pledges to cover living and ministry expenses. It was during this time that our second child, Kara, came along.

This made things even more exhausting, but it was all worth it. Seeds of the gospel were sown, took root and grew. A little less than 19 years later, under a ministry we incorporated by the name of Native American Ministries (NAM), we traveled back to Lower Brule, to build brand new facilities there. The church that grew from those seeds is alive and thriving and now not only supports our ministry, but reaches out to other reservations in South Dakota.

Our ministry in South Dakota began with Sioux Indians, but currently involves more than a dozen churches on reservations stretching from Wisconsin to Arizona. NAM works closely with pastors and their congregations to assist them with everything from developing long-term institutional plans and hosting community events that draw as many as 2,000 Indians, to construction projects and leadership training. Through two auxiliary programs, we supply backpacks full of school supplies and Christmas boxes. We also provide thousands of dollars worth of children's and adult Bibles as well as recovery Bibles. The recovery Bibles help the churches develop alcohol and drug abuse support groups in a faith-based environment.

This is especially important because social chaos exists on many of the reservations across this land. Because of this, alcoholism has become the main opiate to deal with all of the resultant pain and feelings of despair. Along with widespread alcoholism come all of the violence, neglect, and abuse associated with it. I understand this.

In addition to my own struggle with alcoholism, there was a period of time in my life, as a result of the accident, when I found myself, for the most part, locked into a welfare system. I had money to spend from Supplemental Social Security and from an insurance settlement, but I did not have to work for it. What I possessed was a bad combination of cash and a lot of free time, but no meaningful work. I did what many people in this predicament do – I got into a lot of trouble. My life was not constructive. I did not contribute to the needs of my parents, even though I was living under their roof. I was lying around, smoking dope, and getting drunk. I had nothing to take pride in and I had nothing that gave me a sense of accomplishment.

Many Native Americans find themselves imprisoned by this nation's welfare system in a similar way. The system itself is, in my opinion, a cruel scourge on this land. It robs a man of his dignity, chains him to the shackles of poverty, and drives him into compulsive/addictive behaviors in order to cope with this beast.

As ministers among the Native Americans, we serve a people who are misunderstood, who are familiar with death and dying, who often face nearly impossible situations, and who are deeply scarred by life experiences. Culturally, they are torn between tradition and Anglo worldviews. Socially, everything has been turned upside down. Native

Americans were originally a people typified as moral and family-oriented, with a well-developed judicial system and devotion to worshiping their deity(s). Although these ideals are still verbalized by the tribes, the ability to live these lofty "codes" of life on the reservations steadily escapes the grasp of most.

Over the years we have come to realize that the most powerful ministry we can have to the Native Americans is to resource the vision of reservation pastors by partnering with them to empower their own people. We work with each ministry for three to five years, providing the resources they need to become strong, self-sustaining works that are eventually able to initiate and sustain ministry beyond their own communities.

This approach is effective. As noted earlier, the Lower Brule church went from nearly being closed down to now having new facilities and ministries that reach beyond their own community. We have facilitated the renovation of several others. A pastor from the Fort Apache Reservation asked us to help him develop his children's program and it grew by approximately 50 children the first year alone. We staged fun community events and outreaches that opened doors and built the trust needed to share Christ while at the same time planted seeds of transformation and hope in these downtrodden Native American communities. Watching those seeds grow and blossom into changed lives and strong native churches that are transforming their own communities has been an indescribable pleasure.

Through our work with NAM, we have gained a new extended family. These people and the rugged terrain of their native lands have become as much a part of our soul as blood relatives. I love these people, and I love their land. We have come to feel as if we are one with them. Our work with the

Native American people has taught me that a meaningful life isn't about perfect good looks, financial security, or being admired by the masses. It is about receiving and sharing the love of God and passing on the life-changing power of salvation in Jesus Christ. Fullness of life is about compassion for the hurting, mercy for the fallen, charity for all mankind. True Christian life is about caring for your neighbor, even if it is at great expense to yourself. Most of my neighbors just happen to live hundreds of miles away in the most impoverished areas of the United States.

By the time I had reached my late 30s, I felt like I had surely paid all the dues life required, and I did not live in fear of future catastrophes. I felt they were a thing of the past. But life is like a major league pitcher. It has a plentiful supply of curveballs and a real strong arm. Seemingly out of nowhere, I was about to step up to the plate once again, and this ball was the one that threatened to take me out of the game.

Chapter 17

A HIDDEN ENEMY

"True hope dwells on the possible, even when life seems to be a plot written by someone who wants to see how much adversity we can overcome. True hope responds to the real world, to real life; it is an active effort." ~ *Walter Anderson*

"Kc Kopaska: survivor." That's how I saw myself, and everyone I knew considered this a great sign of success. I had survived a childhood with a raging, abusive father, a mind-numbing accident that left me with third degree burns over nearly 60 percent of my body, years of hardcore drug and alcohol abuse, a stint in a psychiatric hospital, and intense ministerial conflicts, even life-threatening challenges on the reservations. Surely by this time, disaster was in my past, and I was desensitized to the possibility of another monster tribulation.

As I neared 40 years of age, I started thinking about my health and decided that when I turned 40, I would make an appointment to get a routine physical exam. I did not feel ill; it just seemed like a wise thing to do. During the course of the physical, the doctor asked me if I wanted a blood screening for AIDS and Hepatitis C Virus (HCV). I felt almost embarrassed when he asked me because of the stigma attached to AIDS. Nonetheless, I responded with a shrug of the shoulders, saying, "Sure, might as well." I did not expect any positive results from the tests.

Several weeks later he called me back to his office to discuss the results. The report came back negative on AIDS, but positive on HCV. My doctor gave me the news with little emotion, and I received it much the same way, though I wondered how I had contracted the disease. Our best guess was that I was infected by the blood transfusions at Brooke. Since the transfusions had been in 1976, the doctor suggested a liver biopsy in order to determine how far the disease had progressed.

The biopsy determined that there was scarring in my liver. Still, I was not alarmed since I thought that the scarring could have been caused by my former substance abuse instead of the disease. Soon after the biopsy, another consultation was scheduled and I was informed of my treatment options. There were only two – to start treatment now, or take a "wait and see" approach. I chose the latter, reasoning, "Why make myself sick treating a disease that did not make me feel ill to begin with?" There were, however, other significant reasons for my delay.

Treatment for HCV consisted of a weekly, self-administered injection of a chemical called *peginterferon alfa* and a daily oral ingestion of another chemical called *ribavirin* for a period of at least 12 months. The treatment was comparable to being treated with two types of chemotherapy at the same time for 12 months, complete with many of chemo's side effects. As a matter of fact, *interferon* is also used to treat cancer. There was no way in the world I was going to rush into that. Despite the dangers of the disease, I tabled the idea for about another four years.

That was probably not a very good idea.

Though it is not commonly known, HCV kills 10,000 to 20,000 Americans a year and is a leading cause of cirrhosis, liver cancer, and liver failure. It is also the leading cause of liver transplants in this country. It is theoretically incurable, meaning that the goal of treatment is simply to get the virus in remission. I had contracted the worst genotype or, put another way, the most difficult strain to treat. This further complicated my decision since there was less than a 40 percent chance of successful treatment and a 60 percent chance of reoccurrence within two years. The side effects of the chemicals were more disconcerting to me than being infected by a potentially fatal disease. I put it out of my mind. Providing for my family and developing a ministry were enough to occupy my daily thoughts and activities.

Four years passed by after my initial diagnosis before I had a second blood test as part of another routine examination. This test exposed an elevation of liver enzymes, an indicator of the disease's progression. As a result, another biopsy was scheduled, the results of which showed a definite increase in liver scarring. The choice of whether or not to get treatment became a little more serious.

After much deliberation with my wife and a physician friend, I finally opted for treatment. Never mind that I was told I would be very sick for a substantial period of time, the worst part was that my doctor ordered me to lighten my workload and slow down until it was over. I did not want to hear this. The doctor didn't seem to realize that I don't have a low gear. Little did any of us know, however, that circumstances beyond anyone's control were about to kick my life into high gear, and there was nothing anyone could do to stop it. I would be forced into overdrive for a good portion of the treatment, exactly when I should have been slowing down. Early in the spring of 2004, I took my first shot and popped my first couple of pills. Then came the hurricanes of 2004.

It was in this season that I was employed by a compassion organization called "Convoy of Hope" as their Director of US Disaster Response and Director of Native American Outreaches. I seem to be a man who needs constant challenges in order to rise to my potential, and this job provided plenty of them! As director, I was to organize and oversee on the ground all of their operations for every major U.S. disaster, and a number of smaller ones. During my four-year tenure in this position, I developed a rapid response system in which I had the ability to order truckloads of supplies en route to an event before it occurred, in the case of hurricanes, or while it was taking place, in the case of massive wild land fires or floods. I taught myself to forecast hurricanes, wildfire activity, and flooding with excellent accuracy. It was a necessity; one mistake could potentially cost the organization thousands of dollars. I did not make many.

2004 was one of the worst hurricane seasons in US history. It started with hurricane Charley, which came ashore at Punta Gorda, Florida on August 14th as a category four storm with maximum sustained winds of 145 miles per hour. Wind gusts were much higher. As I monitored the storm from my office in Springfield, Missouri, I finally decided to get at least one semi load of water en route while it was still well out in the Gulf of Mexico. A truck driver and I arrived in Punta Gorda four hours after the hurricane made landfall. It was a good call. In all, Charley destroyed 25,000 homes and was so strong that it was still clocking winds speeds of 100 mph as far inland as Orlando. There was one huge problem though – I did not have with me the means to monitor Atlantic weather systems and, therefore, did not realize that there were three other hurricanes hot on Charley's heels. I had not brought enough medication to continue my HCV treatment. Besides that, the interferon had to be refrigerated. I was not leaving Florida to get the meds. I don't quit on the job. We would have to find a way to get my meds down south.

Charley was followed by Hurricane Frances, which came ashore at Sewall's Point, on September 5, with 105-mile-an-hour winds, paving the way for Hurricane Ivan. Ivan was the season's monster storm. For two weeks the hurricane thrashed across the Caribbean Sea and Gulf of Mexico, killing dozens and inflicting massive property damage from the Leeward Islands to Cuba. At one point Ivan's winds reached 165 miles an hour, making it one of the strongest hurricanes in recorded history. It weakened considerably before its eye finally came ashore near Mobile Bay, Alabama, on September 16. Not far behind it was another hefty huffer named Jeanne. It moved on shore near Stuart, Florida, near the same place as Frances, as a category three storm, packing maximum sustained winds of 115 mph.

While my crew and I were attending to the needs of the folks in and around Punta Gorda, the Executive Director of Convoy of Hope decided to seize the opportunity for a little public relations and flew down with his media guy for an interview and coverage of our operations. I am glad he did. Diane was able to send with him a plentiful supply of my medications, and since our semi-tractors had refrigerators in the sleeping compartments, I was able to keep them cooled.

The work of tending to the needs of thousands of disaster victims, in the hot Florida sun, for weeks on end finally took its toll. I was already exhausted after the first few days of dealing with Hurricane Charley. We did not have hotels to rest or clean up in and ate when it was convenient, which was not often. The food selection was not all that great either.

My emotional state deteriorated along with my physical condition. The medications began interfering with my brain chemistry, and I noticed that I was experiencing inexplicable mood swings. I thought it was fatigue. Among other brain chemistry issues, my serotonin levels were also thrown out of whack. I later had to be medicated for that as well.

By the time we were wrapping up our response to Jeanne, I was on an airplane en route to the Fort Apache Reservation in Arizona in order to conduct a community outreach at the village of Cibecue. I was exhausted, but I could not cancel out. The outreach involved too many volunteers from various parts of the country who had planned vacations and their annual mission trips for this occasion.

I wish I could say that it all went off without a hitch, but it did not. The morning of the event, just as I was pulling onto the rodeo grounds with my only helper from Convoy of Hope, the truck driver who delivered the supplies, his phone rang. It was his wife. She called with the news that his daughter and her boyfriend had been found dead, apparently the victims of a drug overdose. I had to quickly assemble a team, unload the truck, and get him on his way. Once that was accomplished, I reassembled the team and prayed, first for him and his grieving family, and then for us. I presented the team with the choice of either letting this put a damper on our spirits, which in turn, would carry over to our guests, or to determine to put on the best event that we could with an attitude of joy and servanthood in honor of our truck driver and his family. The group chose the latter.

These attitude choices made all the difference. Because of their choice to honor God and their colleague by putting on the best event possible, the event was a great success, with at least 600 people from the community showing up. The unity and positive momentum begun that weekend was still changing the community a year later! On the day of the outreach the church's attendance was running at about five people. A year later, the church had added a new building and was running approximately 150 people in attendance.

When I arrived home after the outreach in Cibecue, however, I was mentally and physically spent. I had been away for the better part of six weeks in all, under prolonged, intense stress the entire time. I needed to get away for a while for a little "R and R." My idea of R and R was to go mountain climbing. One of the goals on my bucket list is to climb to the high point of every state in the United States. So this time, I chose King's Peak at 13,528 feet in Utah and Borah Peak at 12,662 feet in Idaho. Though it is ranked the seventh hardest of the 50 highpoints, King's Peak is not a technical climb, just a long one. The hike from the trailhead to the top and back was 28 miles, round trip. I did it in two days.

Borah Peak was a little more challenging. The trail to the peak is steep with few switchbacks and ascends more than 5,200 feet in 3.5 miles. At 11,800 feet I came upon the infamous "Chicken-Out Ridge." A lot of people take one look at it, turn around, and hike back down the mountain. One can literally sit on top of it and straddle it with both legs on either side. As I carefully inched my way along the top of it, I was blocked by a man who was doing just that. In mountaineering terminology, he was "gripped", afraid to make a move.

"Man, you've got to get going or we are going to be trapped up here when the afternoon storms roll in," I said.

"Shut up!" he retorted. "I don't got to do anything except crap and pay taxes!"

Obviously, he wasn't budging any time soon. Somehow, I managed to make my way carefully around him. My next encounter with a person in the "grip" was a woman afraid to down climb the vertical wall at the end of the ridge, which led to a snowfield that was the last significant challenge to the peak. Her "grip" was not without merit. To put it politely, one slip on the narrow path of the snowfield and it's a long way to the bottom. As steep as it was, even with an ice ax, it would have been very difficult to slow one's descent no matter how you took it. Not a pretty fall.

I looked at the frightened woman and said, "Look lady, I don't have any fingers. I'll go first and if I make it than you should be able to." I made it and she did too. I went on to the peak. Borah Peak was not a mountain to be trifled with. As I sat on the peak munching on some snacks, I quietly prayed, "God, I sure would like to see my next birthday." I still had to get down the thing in one piece. Somehow I did, and lived to tell the story.

My logic in going mountain climbing as a means of recovering from the extreme stress of the Florida hurricanes and the Cibecue outreach was not as crazy as it sounds. Here's why – mountain climbing is one of my most cherished pastimes. Surrounded by snowcapped peaks, breathing clean crisp air, for a few hours I have no other world except the mountain. All troubles cease to exist. I always go home refreshed. When I am on the trail, all of life's craziness goes away. It is just me, the beauty of the mountains, and the challenge of the climb. In many cases, the climb commands every bit of my attention which means nothing else exists except the moment.

But for some reason, this time it didn't work. I was too far gone. Treatment was killing my red blood cells faster than my body could regenerate them. Though it felt great being in the mountains again, climbing King's and Borah Peaks took more out of me than it gave back. I didn't know that

I was suffering from anemia, and my emotions were out of control. Even my old friend, the Great Outdoors, couldn't help me this time.

A couple of weeks later, I scheduled a visit with my general physician who put me on meds to help stabilize my emotions. During my monthly exam with my gastrointestinal doctor who was in charge of monitoring my progress and determining the course of treatment, I got a scolding. The doctor took one look at me and said, "Kc, you need to slow down." I knew the only way that would happen was if I took a medical sabbatical from the ministry. This time, there was no second-guessing the decision.

Roughly six months into treatment, side effects had set in, including hair loss, insomnia, loss of appetite with resulting weight loss, extreme fatigue, and painful muscle twitches. My short-term memory suffered significant loss. Eventually, my red blood cell count went so low that my doctor was afraid that he might need to stop the HCV treatment. One day I went to bed and hardly got out for 10 days. During that week and a half I lost another 10 pounds, on top of the 18 that I had already shed, involuntarily. I was just too weak and sick to do anything but lay in bed.

After 10 days, I finally crawled out of bed and shuffled into the living room where Diane was sitting in an easy chair reading a book. I looked at her and said, "I've got to do something about this." That moment became my turning point.

I don't know how it happened, but from somewhere deep down inside I summoned up the will to fight back – to fight back against the sickness, depression, and the extreme fatigue. I had never felt so tired in all my life, not even in the burn center. If this disease was going to take me down, it wasn't going to do so without a fight. I was determined to get healthy again even if it killed me. In the meantime, I had another decision to make.

The time away from Convoy of Hope gave me the opportunity to re-evaluate my ministry. As much as I loved the adrenaline rush of disaster response work, I knew I was not honoring my call to Native American Ministries. While I was busy at Convoy, I was just dabbling at NAM. Without making a big "to-do" about it, I made the decision and resigned my position at Convoy. It was a good decision, but I did not anticipate the emotional backlash that went on inside of me. Now I was not only deathly ill, but I was also without a ministry for the first time in 15 years. Being sick was a familiar foe of which I had absolutely no fear. But not having a ministry, and no clue as to when or what I would be doing in the future? That really rattled my cage.

In fact, I felt completely lost.

Being a "survivor" was no longer enough to help me hit the curve balls in life. I had to move beyond "survival" if I was going to make it the rest of the way.

Chapter 18

THE SWEET PAIN OF VICTORY

I had to beat HCV or it was going to beat me. And if I was going to beat HCV, it would have to be a strategic battle. This disease wasn't going down without a fight, and I planned to give it one. Where exactly was the battleground, though, and what were the weapons? I was already fighting back with chemotherapy and bed rest, following medical wisdom and tradition. But it was not enough. What else could I do?

I am a naturally goal-oriented person. I need goals in my life in order to stay motivated. Before I started treatment for HCV, I had been doing a little bit of running and working out in preparation for the strenuous activity of my favorite passion, mountain climbing. I do not know what possessed me, but one morning I woke up and knew that my battleground for fighting HCV was going to be running. I also knew that my goal for running had to be bigger than my disease. The only goal I could think of that seemed big enough to beat HCV would be to train for a marathon.

For several years I had wondered what it would be like to run a marathon. It was fascinating to me to think that people could run 26.2 miles, in one stint, in close to two hours. Never mind the fact that I could barely get out of bed, did not know how to train for a 26.2 mile race, nor did I possess a decent pair of running shoes. No matter also that I suffered from a diminished appetite and severe anemia from HCV treatments. Whatever. The only thing I knew for sure was that I had to get out of bed and start running, and that it would take a goal the size of a marathon to get me out of bed and on my feet again.

My first attempt at a training run was not very encouraging. Our street is about two blocks long. I could not even run to the end of it and back without taking a walking break. I thought about it and decided that I would set a series of smaller goals. There is an old saying that states, "Inch by inch life's a cinch, but mile by mile it's a trial." I decided to "inch" my way along. The little goals were much more manageable and less overwhelming than planning a huge training program. My first goal was simply to run to the end of the street and back without stopping to walk. My next goal was to train for a month, and determine if I noticed significant improvement in my endurance and mileage enough to keep going. Of course "significant" was a very relevant term when compared to running a couple of blocks.

After a month I was pleased with my improvement but also knew that I had a long way to go. On the other hand, though, training was proving to be much more difficult than I had bargained for. My anemia made it difficult to even get off of the couch in order to walk to the kitchen table and nibble on some food before running, let alone tie up my running shoes and head out the door, especially on cold winter nights. Many times I looked at Diane and said, "I don't want to do this," then did it anyway. I was tired all of the time. Sometimes, I had to fight back tears as I donned my running clothes. But I knew that if I was going to beat this thing, I had to be determined to accomplish this goal of running a marathon.

As utterly miserable as training for a marathon made me, especially while in HCV treatments, it ended up being very therapeutic. I was taking back some control of my life, a primary component to overcoming hardship. Physical training also provided an outlet for all of my mixed up emotions, enabling me to get a better handle on them. Most important of all, it deepened my relationship with God.

When I was out there on those cold winter nights, with no one else around, I often felt His presence in a very real way. There were a few times when I actually looked back over my shoulder to see if someone was there. Though I did not hear any audible voices, I sensed Him telling me not to give up, in running or in the ministry; to keep reaching for my goal. It was as though He had slipped on a pair of His own running shoes and was out there trotting right along with me. These were priceless moments. All of my suffering was worth it just to experience that kind of closeness with God.

After a couple of months of training, I found myself at a plateau where I was neither gaining mileage nor speed. I needed initiative. I did a little research on races around the country and ran across the Deadwood Mickelson Trail Marathon in the Black Hills of South Dakota. It was scheduled for June 5th, a miniscule three weeks after my last treatment. I would still be recovering from that, and I would still be anemic. It took a lot of nerve, but I summoned up the courage, or the insanity, to send in my fee and register anyway. In my mind, once that was accomplished, there was no turning back. Entering a marathon race was such a crazy thing to do. Most people who are treated for HCV are happy just to have survived the ordeal and expect to experience side effects long after it is over. But I wasn't content to be "most people." I wanted my health back, and that meant going the extra mile, literally. I had to become "more than a conqueror" as Romans 8:37 says, to have a chance at full recovery.

Deadwood Mickelson Trail Marathon is not an easy race course. The first 13 miles of the route involved a slight upgrade. The second half was more or less slightly downhill. Running downhill trashes the quads. Even crazier was the fact that there would be a major altitude change. The Mickelson's elevation sits at 5,787.4 feet, while my home and training ground sits at a mere 1,300 feet. Yet another challenge for my anemic body!

I needed a "motivator" to set my mind on and push myself toward, so I decided to motivate myself with the "Cause" of overcoming HCV. I even designed a logo that said, "Overcoming HCV one mile at a time." and had an iron-on decal made for my running shirt. This seemed to be a great idea, until we encountered just one little problem. Diane accidentally ironed the decal on upside down. She felt terrible about it but there wasn't anything that could be done to fix it. I knew that finishing the marathon was as much a "mind game" as a physical one, and I became truly worried that I might not be able to pull it off now that I had lost my "Cause" t-shirt.

When I awoke on the morning of the marathon, I was still worried about how I was going to motivate myself to run strong for 26.2 miles. The longest I had run in my training was 14 miles. My "Cause," the thing I dreamed about and had sometimes even become "teary" about while training on countless lonely roads, was now gone with the misalignment of a single decal. I admit I was being overly dramatic at that moment, but at the time every little stumbling block seemed like a mountainous obstacle to be overcome.

The starting line of the race was in front of a small church in a tiny Black Hills town called Rochford. The atmosphere was not what I had imagined. Instead of runners stretching, warming up, and jockeying for position, they were clamoring for a place to relieve themselves before the start of the race. The line to the port-o-potties was impossibly long. Those of us who remembered the good old days of outhouses got into a very short line in front of the one that was behind the church. Quite a few runners, women included, said, "forget it" and ran up a nearby hill to water the trees. I peed, drank water, slurped on some energy gel, and tried to keep from getting too cold. It finally dawned on me that I could go inside the small church to warm up by attending their church service.

I wasn't the first runner with this bright idea. The little building was packed pew-to-pew and wall-to-wall with runners! It was kind of funny. I know that this little church had never seen so many people stuffed inside of it before. They were all there for only one reason — to stay warm! Otherwise, most of these runners never visited a church except for funerals and weddings. That poor preacher! He had a church full of runners decked out in running shorts with tiny pockets, and not much to contribute to the offering. On top of that, it is doubtful that many people's minds were on the sermon. Still, he conducted the service bravely and sincerely. As I stepped back outside into the cool morning air after the service and got ready to line up, I was acutely aware of having very little emotion about the run. I didn't know what to expect.

I was near the back of the pack when the starting gun went off. Nearly 500 runners went bobbing down the trail in front of me. It was an incredible sight to see so many people, dressed in all kinds of colorful running apparel, jockeying for position in the bright sunshine of a Black Hills morning. I felt a thrill rush through me. I set my pace at about the speed of a three-legged turtle.

Several miles into the race, my mind began playing tricks on me, once again telling me I could never complete the run without my "Cause" t-shirt. Finally I fought back. "Forget the stupid cause," I told myself. "I'll be my own cause. I'll run for the Kc Kopaska cause!" Once I declared this mentally, I felt good about the idea, and began to relax. Steadily, I settled into my slow plod toward Deadwood.

As I persevered, a sense of peacefulness and gratitude rose up in me and crowded out the past 12 months of sickness, uncertainty, and despair. I felt deeply blessed to be out on the trail and doubts that I could not finish the race began to fade away. The George Mickelson Trail was made out of an old railroad line that ran for 110 miles from Deadwood to Edgemont through the beautiful Black Hills of South Dakota. I was in my element, outdoors and on the move, running through pine forests, over crystal clear streams, and along bright green patches of open grasslands. All of the cares of life vanished. My old friend the Great Outdoors was back, lending his strength and running with me, drowning out the cares of life with a chorus of singing birds, gurgling brooks, and whispering pines.

When I passed the 14-mile marker it occurred to me that I was about to run farther than I have ever run at any one time. It was a small milestone en route to an even greater one, but at that point, I began to struggle. I did not know how many carbohydrates to eat or at what rate to eat them prior to and during the race. It wasn't long before I was running out of fuel and hurting, too. I kept pushing about as hard as I could until the 22-mile mark, then I hit "the wall." My trudging plod slowed to a painful walk for the next two miles. My feet hurt, my quads were on fire, and my knees ached. The next 4.2 miles seemed impossibly long. I was completely out of energy as I walked painfully, barely putting one foot in front of the other. Then, with just a little over two miles left to go, something wonderful happened. I found a second wind. Now there was no way I was going to walk across the finish line. Somehow, I determined to finish the marathon running, however fast my poor little old legs could carry me.

With the "second wind" energy coursing through my veins, I ran across the finish line at 5:40. It was a slow time, but the time did not matter. Crossing the finish line did.

When I ran through that timing gate, I was completely spent. Quickly, I found a place to sit down and did not move for several minutes. There to greet me were my wonderful wife, two of her sisters, and her parents. When I finally managed to stand up again, it was to hobble back to the car and get something to eat. Barely able to walk, everything in my body throbbed in pain; but it was a wonderful kind of pain. This was not the pain of sickness and defeat; it was the pain of sacrifice and perseverance that accompanies all great accomplishments. It was pain sweetened by victory.

Instead of giving in to HCV, I had fought back and won. The disease did not beat me, nor did the side effects of treatment. Something in me changed the day I crossed that finish line. I no longer felt like just a survivor; now I felt like a conqueror. Crossing the finish line of the Deadwood Mickelson Trail Marathon was not the end of the race for me. In fact, it was just the beginning.

WISDOM IN SUFFERING

"Today I know that ...the (hard) experiences of our lives, when we let God use them, become the mysterious and perfect preparation for the work He will give us to do." ~ Corrie Ten Boom, Holocaust survivor, speaker and author

There is wisdom in suffering, the kind of wisdom that clarifies the lenses of our rose-colored glasses and allows us to more accurately see the world as it is. The world we live in is a painful one.

There are those who make it their life's pursuit to take hold of a worry-free existence, spending their time, energy and money on ways to be sheltered from trials. They seek a life full of personal peace, affluence and self-satisfaction. I understand that. Who wouldn't want a perfect life? In fact, a person would have to be mentally imbalanced to not want this. But the sad truth is that such a life simply does not exist on this planet.

After the accident, when my skin toughened up and I was able to drive and become more independent, I thought the answer to life was to make it into one big party. Instead of a worry-free existence, however, I found myself in more and more trouble with the law. I drank and did drugs very heavily. It was not uncommon for me to get all cranked up on amphetamines for several days on end, or to drink around the clock. This provided only temporary escapes from pain and emptiness, though, and often caused more pain to deal with later.

None of this was new to me at this point in my life. I was already into hard liquor and drugs such as PCP, LSD and pharmaceutical drugs by the age of 13. If none of these drugs was available, and sometimes even if they were, I would inhale any vaporous substances I thought would make me high. My rebellious lifestyle, including drug abuse and bouts with the law, was symptomatic of a young man running from the things that hurt him instead of accepting them and dealing with them. I needed to confront the unresolved conflict and grief in my life but I did not know how. That is, until Jesus Christ took over my life.

What Jesus Christ had to work with was a burned up, burned out individual, locked away in a psychiatric center, who had not done a single thing with his life except indulge it with bitterness and anger. I was a wretched, insecure, hopeless little man making one last attempt at grasping hold of life itself.

There was an immediate emotional healing that took place in my life at the point of my salvation, but there was also a great deal of additional healing that took place over the years and through many circumstances, good and bad. It may seem paradoxical to a life of faith, but God, for me, has been a "realist" who has helped me most through support and confrontation. Simply put, I had to square off with what ailed me. There would be no more running, no more escaping, even through "Christian" dependencies, such as legalism, self-righteous anger, the ministry itself, or "admirable" workaholism. A truly powerful, overcoming life in Jesus Christ is a life of confrontation, first of all, with one's self. I had to face myself; I had to face what hurt.

There are no quick-fix solutions to healing the invisible scars of the human psyche. Getting saved is not enough, getting baptized in the Holy Spirit will not cure you, and all the altar calls in the world are powerless to reach the inner man if a person is unwilling to face himself as he really is. Christians have different names for this – total surrender, rededication, yielding everything in our lives to the Holy Spirit. But whatever it is called, it means we take down our guard before God and give Him permission to deal with us. This can be a very painful (and sometimes frightening) thing to allow.

When facing past abuses, molestations, broken families, the loss of a loved one, and other realities of this fallen world, we have to first admit our struggles. Then we have to let go of them and take hold of something better – Jesus Christ, and His new direction for our life. Human forgiveness, positive affirmations, and love bring much healing to us, but only Jesus gives new life.

Through Jesus, my scars were transformed from reminders of tragedy and loss to doorways of opportunity and growth. My scars made me more compassionate, more humble, and in many ways led me to the wonderful life I have today. I am thankful for my scars now, not ashamed of them. They have become a source of strength.

I had to come to the place where I accepted the things in my life that hurt me, and the fact that I would be dramatically disfigured the rest of my life because of someone else's carelessness. I also had to accept all of the injustices and mistreatment I had suffered from a multitude of people, and let go of bitter attitudes and desires for revenge or judgment.

When I did finally face these situations, and determined to move on with my life in spite of it all, a wonderful healing began to take place in my life.

ABOUT THE AUTHORS...

About Kc Kopaska...

One tragedy is enough to knock the wind of life out of a person while others experience multiple tragedies and keep on going. That is Kc Kopaska. Kc survived the debilitating sting of extreme family dysfunction, a near fatal accident, the grueling process of burn victim recovery, substance abuse , alcoholism, and many years later, fought his way back to life from an incurable disease.

Kc knows first hand the gut wrenching nature of personal tragedy, but he also knows how to not only survive it, but also how to use tragedy to transform life for the better.

Kc lives in Republic, Missouri, with his wife, Diane, and has two grown children, Cody and Kara, a Son-in-Law, Nathan Murphy, and two worthless mutts named Remington and Macey.

He works with pastors on Native American reservations all across the United States in order to assist their efforts to improve the lives of some of the most impoverished people in America. He is also an active fire chaplain for the Clever Fire District located near his hometown.

Kc holds an MA in Biblical Literature and an M.Div. in Missiology. He is certified with the International Critical Incident Stress Foundation in Mass Disasters and Terrorism.

About co-author, Carole Liston...

Carole Liston is an award winning freelance writer, photographer, and writing teacher. She specializes in writing inspirational stories based on the true experiences of ordinary people who have overcome extraordinary circumstances through faith, courage, and unstoppable determination.

Carole holds a degree in communications and has published over 300 feature articles on award winning persons and businesses. She has three books scheduled to go to press this year. In addition to her freelance work, she enjoys teaching writing in local colleges and volunteering with regional youth. She resides with her family and a three legged cat named "Almost" in Joplin, Missouri.

ADDITIONAL RESOURCES

Additional Information about Kc Kopaska
and his Ministries can be found at:

www.nativeamerican-ministries.org

CPSIA information can be obtained at www.ICGtesting.com
Printed in the USA
236723LV00002B/2/P